Beyond Angels

Beyond Angels

An Enlightenment Revealed

A calling to the New-Age movement
to adopt a consciousness-first approach
to its healing and meditation practices

Gaile Walker

BOOKS

Winchester, UK
Washington, USA

First published by O-Books, 2013
O-Books is an imprint of John Hunt Publishing Ltd., Laurel House, Station Approach,
Alresford, Hants, SO24 9JH, UK
office1@jhpbooks.net
www.johnhuntpublishing.com

For distributor details and how to order please visit the 'Ordering' section on our website.

ISBN: 978 1 84694 839 8

A CIP catalogue record for this book is available from the British Library.

Design: Stuart Davies

Printed and bound by CPI Group (UK) Ltd, Croydon, CR0 4YY

To Mum and Dad
for giving me the freedom to be me.

"The book you are compiling now will talk of the Mother's light, when asked if you have it you must respond yes... You must speak of the dangers... You must speak of your awakening to show the possibilities... You must talk of the way the Mother's heart bleeds to see suffering, show God's compassion in action. You must dance with the Mother, dance to my tune, sing my song, spread my light in your world."

Mother Divine
2000

CONTENTS

Acknowledgements

This book could not have emerged in the shape that it is without the assistance of the following: Paul Mason for his help with the referencing and Alistair Shearer for his advice on structure. Wendy Kraft, Andy Cowan and Sheila Hakin for their comments. Ingrid St Clare for introducing me to the beautiful technique that is 'The Radiance Technique®' and Shoshana Shay for her help with the registered service marks. My 'TM teacher', Rowan Barnden, for bringing her teaching to our doorstep. Dominic Mitchell for his insight and longstanding friend June Clarke for her early encouragement. Sue Kerley for her trust and Tricia Sterry for her commitment. Dr. Roger Chalmers for helping me understand that expression was my physical pathway, David Ellis for reminding me it was a duty and JJ for her story. June Keeble, Sue Jenkinson, Bryan Austin and Chrissy Smith for their unfailing commitment to the meditation group and the invaluable discussions and suggestions. Ricarda Erbse, the kindest of friends, for teaching me that I should give thanks for what I could see.

Endless thanks to my family: accepting supportive parents and the best sister ever, for their love, patience and generosity. And to my partner, who in his own special way has kept my feet firmly on the ground and helped more than he knows.

'Jai* Guru Dev' for preparing Maharishi Mahesh Yogi to leave isolation and reach out to the Western world. My heartfelt thanks to my savior Maharishi Mahesh Yogi whose light in the world relieved the suffering of so many. And to Dr. Barbara Ray whose teaching expanded my vision further.

With deepest gratitude and inexpressible thanks to Mother Divine in all her physical forms. For Her unconditional love, suffering, endless darshan and gift of compassionate Grace. It is Her light alone which supports us. She is God in human form.

*All glory and thanks go to…

The Emergence of a Hermit

I

Introduction

The sharing of experience is one of the most unifying principles of this physical world. It has taken me years of systematic inner and outer investigation to be able to share this book with you. I practiced Transcendental Meditation™ (usually known as TM) as taught by Maharishi Mahesh Yogi, for 37 years. I have also learned the exceptional healing and meditation technique called The Radiance Technique®, Authentic Reiki®, Real Reiki® and TRT®, which is taught by Dr. Barbara Ray, Ph.D. (The word healing is used here in the sense of coming to feel inwardly fulfilled and complete.) At the time of publishing I have benefited from using TRT® for 17 years (learning in 1995) and have studied it to The Sixth Degree. I am also an Authorized Instructor of The First and Second Degrees of The Radiance Technique®, Authentic Reiki®. Despite this I do not intend to write about this technique. Dr. Barbara Ray, Ph.D. is the holder of all the intact keys of this system and as such is the only expert. Nor do I intend to write about Transcendental Meditation™. Although asked, I never became a teacher of TM. Maharishi Mahesh Yogi was, however, my first teacher, his explanations gave words to my spiritual experience and it is these experiences I wish to share. In this book I also relate my understanding of topics that interest me as a transcendental light healer and transcendental meditator. Included is my own personal theory of healing and views on the process of spiritual development. My wish is to highlight the importance and efficacy, as I personally see them, of Transcendent teachings in general and to encourage all seekers, meditators and healers to use them. It is my intention to encourage healers to become more enquiring and informed about what they do. I also hope to persuade those who make up the New-Age movement to reassess their practices, with a view to incorporating within them a Transcendent connection, and so adopt a 'consciousness-first' approach to their healing.

The upsurge in New-Age teaching and the fact that it is now possible to talk openly about the power of thought and the existence of consciousness is obviously a reflection of some change in the collective awareness. It seems to me, however, that much of the present New-Age teaching is, at most, an introduction to the subject of spirituality; usually it is not discriminating, at worst it could be described as complacent. Generally it leaves the reader with the impression that their spiritual evolution is automatic and inevitable. Determination and persistence, in connection with spiritual development, are not words which feature heavily in the New-Age arena. The word suffering is one that does. Just before writing this introduction I read yet another undirected New-Age article which talks of how we should gain spiritual development from our times of suffering. Perhaps, but what exactly is spiritual development and how do we gain from painful experience? Furthermore, why should spiritual development only be attained through suffering? There is currently an attitude to illness which has reached a point that is almost a celebration, illness often being seen as the only way to achieve higher awareness. My aim is to explain what the experience of spiritual evolution is. I hope also to encourage a means of achieving it which is both fast and effective and does not depend on painful experience. There is today a tendency to rush towards the latest sensational healing technique without discernment, the speed with which people become reiki 'masters' is testimony to this, but it is time now for the New-Age movement to become discriminating. I recently read an article about a reiki technique which claims that dolphins are 'masters' and I am left in no doubt that the exalted spiritual status of the title Master is not understood and needs further explanation.

The New-Age movement coupled with the use of scientific enquiry has brought us to the point where the mind-body connection is well documented. The result of this is a teaching which encourages techniques which use the mind (very often through visualization) with the intention of changing unwanted emotions and thoughts. In the same way that opinion polls and the media both reflect and influence public opinion, such therapy can exert a certain influence for well-being. Physical forms, in the shape of bodies, minds or emotions, are a reflection of individual consciousness and there is nothing wrong with working on these directly. This will influence behavior. Invariably, however, the effort this demands outweighs any gain it brings. Time-consuming mental and physical exercises which, even when effective, often produce only temporary change. The mind can be reset to produce a desired behavior, just as a clock can be realigned to tell the correct time. But faulty mechanics or inaccurate resetting will result in a repeated loss of accuracy, and so be of little benefit. The result of this sort of healing is a huge amount of endeavor for too little gain and, more often than not, the physical benefits are not a reflection of spiritual expansion. The physical form of the body is not flexible and is habitual in its behavior. It is therefore difficult to change it when not using techniques which influence outer behavior from further within, from a level more pure and powerful. From the level of Transcendence. It is only through an immersion in Transcendence that a change of consciousness, and so spiritual evolution, will be easily effected. When I have seen other methods which claim to be profound, such as energetic healing, the techniques of healing used have invariably been those that are taught in spiritual healing circles and, as I hope to show, these practices may not be so profound or pure. Changes in thought or behavior, which do not emanate from a change of consciousness, are ineffective in terms of spiritual development. I have attended endless workshops, enticed by the desire to hear about the latest type of healing, always with a new, more effective sounding name. I have listened to speakers describing these 'new' methods only to find that they were still spiritual healing, packaged in a more alluring way. It is the limitations of these methods that I wish to address in this book and I intend to explore the difference that adopting a consciousness-first methodology will make to all New-Age practices.

My purpose is to teach about Transcendence and its value. Nevertheless, it is not my intention to say that any healing which is not completely and directly from the Transcendent is not positive. Nor do I wish to suggest that a healing which may be less helpful is bad. I also do not want to imply that healing should only be undertaken if it is done perfectly; there is always something to be gained and understood. After all, only one teaching would appeal to only one audience, and clearly there are many of both. I do, however, wish to shed some light on the mechanics of healing and meditating, and to particularly show all healers that there is more for them to offer their clients and themselves. I have learned that ultimately spiritual healing, and also many other sorts of healings, are nothing more than the display of the healer's state of being. I have also learned that the limitations of this state of being can be overcome by the use of pure Transcendent systems. Furthermore, the Transcendent system can become a positive addition to any other healing practice.

The New-Age movement, with its predictions of unprecedented leaps in consciousness and physical world changes in 2012, has given the impression that spiritual development is an inevitable clinical process and individuals have little to do. The result of this is complacency. It is true that there is an inner progression which is unfolding in the universe, creating more and more possibilities for an ascent in awareness. But creating possibilities is only one side of a double-sided picture. There is always a choice to be exercised. The New-Age movement is full of the teaching of individual choice and there is a contradiction here. If we have free will and choice, nothing can be inevitable. Suggesting that there is choice must also suggest there is self-responsibility; if there is one, there has to be the other. Exercising the choice to be complacent does not result in an increase of awareness, but in suffering: the very suffering that the New-Age movement claims is spiritually developing.

What my experience has taught me is that, of the many spiritual healers and reiki healers I have met, the dominant view is that one should not express the opinion that a certain sort of healing may not be so helpful or safe. Within the healing circles I have encountered it has been prohibited to suggest that some healing may be more spiritually supportive than others. Views such as these are deemed inexpressible in an environment which claims that all healing is the same and where the meditation and healing technique practiced is predominantly one thing: visualization. I have been vilified by spiritual healers for proposing that there is a safer, more evolutionary practice than the 'channeling of energy'; by reiki practitioners for suggesting that their practice lacked a Transcendent connection; and by some members of a large meditation movement for my use of the word transcendental in relation to the type of healing that I am doing. At present I plough a very lonely furrow in the healing arena when I say that there is no such thing as healing and meditation, only healings and meditations. More so when I contend that illness and distress are not essential parts of the process and that determination and persistence *are* essential for the permanent change of full spiritual development.

It may be helpful to the reader to explain in which context I use several words and expressions:

- It is customary to use capital letters with many of the words in this book. I have resisted this and limited it to a few despite the fact that all words for the Transcendent are deserving of this status. Please take it as read that wherever I use a word to describe the Divine Transcendent the emotion behind the use of capitals exists. I have used 'Self' to denote Transcendent Divine Self and 'self' to describe the physical self. In the desire to make the text easier on the reader's eye I have also used capital letters for some words and expressions such as New-Age. On occasions in place of the words 'he' and 'she' I have put 'they'.

- I have deliberately avoided the use of the words 'soul' and 'higher self' because of the confusion that already exists around them.

- I adopt the words 'effort' and 'determination' to refer to the persistence and time given to realize a goal. I do not mean effort within meditation, quite the opposite. The easier the meditation procedure is, the more effective it will be.

- When I use the word 'evolution' it is in the sense of spiritual development. A growth in awareness of inner levels of existence. The integration of increasingly more refined vibrations of the physical leading towards, and eventually resulting in, the incorporation of Transcendence into individual awareness.

- I realize that my use of the term 'New-Age' movement may appear a little dated to some readers, but it still seems to be a relevant 'umbrella title' for the many mind-body-spirit practices which have emerged from it and are now prevalent in mainstream society.

- It could be argued that there is a difference between the words 'awareness' and 'consciousness'. Awareness exists in animals as well as humans. Animals know where their food is, who gives them it, who loves them and who does not. Even without exalted spiritual development any individual exhibits a certain amount of watchfulness, or awareness. Human awareness can be limited, spiritual understanding predominantly intellectual, or it can grow to incorporate Transcendent Awareness. Humans can become individually conscious of the development of their own Self-awareness in a way in which animals cannot. The limited capacity of animals does not allow them to deliberately raise their own consciousness. For the purposes of this book awareness and consciousness are interchangeable. When I refer to either of the two words it implies both a growth of inner, watchful awareness and an individual becoming conscious of the process.

- I use the words 'Divine' and 'God'. For me they are the most suitable words to describe the experiences I have had, but if these words offend you, please, do use your own.

I am not a writer and, with respect to this, I hope the reader will be forgiving. I write because I have a message. This book is for anyone interested in meditation, healing, psychic abilities and spiritual development. My interest is in healing, of the self, others and the world in which we reside. I believe that all healers have a responsibility to look at their healing practice and to incorporate within it the purest vibration possible. My main interest is in Self-realization, and because of the awakening message within this book, I am hopeful it will spread. It is a message which provides descriptions of expanded states of consciousness and speaks of the fastest means of achieving them. It encourages readers to understand that, given enough time, determination and spiritual practice, it is within their grasp to realize the most elevated spiritual state. That of living full enlightenment.

2

Towards a Book

Growing up as an anxious and unsettled child I had one memorable psychic experience at the age of 7. I saw cherubs in the sky. I heard their music. It has taken over 40 years for me to understand what that experience meant. Always unsatisfied, my search for 'something' began when I was young. Taking myself to church aged 14, I was left with the impression that one hour a week of 'cleansing' was not enough, that an immersion into Divine thought and Grace had to be lived permanently. At 17, I started to investigate meditation techniques. In the year that it took me to search I saw, and rejected, many which sounded sensational but lacked substance. The technique I chose was Transcendental Meditation™ as taught by Maharishi Mahesh Yogi (TM). It was a momentous decision for me, the beginning of a process of rapid Self-discovery. After my first meditation with TM I wasn't shouting its beneficial effects from the rooftops, but I quietly knew, despite this technique being the least 'flashy' of those I had looked at, that if there was such a thing as peace of mind it would help me achieve it.

At the beginning of my twenty-third year on extended meditation courses, inwardly I experienced my first conscious awareness of the presence of Mother Divine: the feminine aspect of the infinite. The feeling that a baby has when being cradled in the arms of its mother was overwhelming. Prior to this I had been aware of the nearness of both a male and a neutral force of nature, formless and omnipresent, but the experience of the Mother became a significant and consistent feature of my life. At that time I had my first experiences of other expanded (or higher) states of awareness. Later that year I slipped into what, in Christopher Isherwood's book, the Avatar Ramakrishna[1] called "Nirvikalpa Samadhi": a state of complete union where there is no distinction between cosmic and individual awareness. (Descriptions of these states of consciousness are given in Chapter 11.) My experiences of these states of consciousness were impossible to doubt and returned for extended periods. Moments of cosmic awareness resulted in a complete identification with Transcendence alongside film-like visions of my past, present and future. These became regular early in 1993 following a consultation with a Maharishi Jyotishee. Vedic[2] incantations over my life-chart, and their predictions of my possibilities, ensured it was an event which signified an important divide between my old life and new.

While meditating in 1993 I quite unexpectedly discovered I could heal through my hands. Waking up in the early hours of the morning I found my young nephew laying on the floor, poorly, suffering from a stomach-related illness he had caught on a family holiday. His father had also contracted it. I sat with him, put my hands on his head, meditated, and he fell asleep. We were all amazed to find that on waking he had recovered, unlike his father who remained unwell for days afterwards. Intrinsically wary about the problems I felt spiritual healing could engender, I did not practice it after this experience, preferring to read around the subject. However, a connection had been made in my mind, although unclear, between Transcendence and a 'hands-on healing'. From my study I formed the opinion that if an individual was spiritually evolved (I mean by this was able to maintain a consistent awareness of Transcendence) they could probably, on their own, create a secure spiritual healing practice. My benchmark was always a combination of Maharishi's teaching and my own experience. Somewhere inside me, though not yet clear, I felt there must be a safe and effective technique which worked on the level of Transcendence and could be used specifically for helping others. I examined numerous techniques called reiki which did not satisfy me. What I saw was an array of different systems, none of which gave me the confidence to attempt them. In fact, I have yet to find a technique simply called reiki which I consider to have a Transcendent capacity. Some that I investigated introduced a very low vibration for healing. I am able to sense vibrations and often to see them as physical objects. At a recent workshop a demonstration was given of a reiki which claimed to attune to sea mammals. As this healing was given I saw a murky energy being pulled upwards from the floor. The person being healed was surrounded by what looked like long grey ribbons, strands of energy, standing as though they were being blown upwards by a fan. They encircled the person being healed. It was quite obvious to me that a dense vibration was being connected to in the name of reiki healing. The range of treatments given under the name of reiki is vast. There are reikis to connect to angels and others to animals; I have even heard of someone having their nose massaged and it being called reiki and recently I saw a reiki for better sex. Furthermore, the speed with which people became so-called reiki 'masters' alarmed me.

My long search ended when I found The Radiance Technique®, Authentic Reiki®, the complete, intact system consisting of seven degrees; rediscovered by Dr. Usui, passed to Dr. Hayashi, Hawayo Takata and directly to Dr. Barbara Ray. The teacher was confident that I would recognize the same Transcendent capacity that I knew from my, then 22, years of practicing TM and all its advanced techniques. A knowing within led me to be certain that, for the first time, I had found a technique worthy of trying. I began to study it in 1995, learning the first of the seven degrees. I have never looked back. Prior to finding The Radiance Technique® I would not have thought that anything could expand upon my practice of that time. What I found was a technique which changed my power of touch, rendering it no longer a reflection of my own level of spiritual development but of Transcendence. I gained a touch which directly activated a Transcendent vibration, not only within me but in the person I touched. This vibration created a healing which went beyond my individual capacity. It activated the vibration of 'wholeness' within the other person too, helping them to be more inwardly aware. I discovered further that the possibility existed to utilize this vibration, to direct it beyond space and time in order to support events, past, present or future. This was without the need for physical touch. I have since come to believe that such an addition to any other form of healing practice is essential. Each and every one of us gives service to others, some through the raising of children and the jobs we undertake, some as healers. This service to society can be transformed into spiritual service through such a Transcendent, spiritually expanding technique as The Radiance Technique®. During my first healing session with The Radiance Technique®, I moved from a place of outward lack of direction, to knowing that I had used it before. I gained an instant understanding that healing with it should be my work in this lifetime. Since studying The First Degree I have been daily helping others with The Radiance Technique®. All my time of connecting to Transcendence had supplied me with the wisdom that there must be more available than what was being offered by the many other practices I had looked at. Those I had seen previously used numerous different vibrations, predominantly physical, which rarely led to the Transcendent. It had taken me 2 years of searching before I found a Transcendent, truly 'wholing' and so truly healing technique which could be used not only for myself but for the benefit of others.

For years in meditation I would regularly see a picture of the solar system, the planets that have been discovered so far in a line from the sun to the outer regions. At the top above the sun would appear 'Transcendence', near the outer planets 'reiki and spiritual healing'. The words I heard were "worlds apart". I always knew they were not the same, I could feel the vibrations, but it has taken me several years of observation to be able to describe this difference. I knew any Transcendent healing practice could not be surpassed. Despite this, and at the time not understanding quite why, I undertook a nationally recognized spiritual healing course. I now know that what I was there to learn was the difference between what spiritual healers were doing and what the possibilities were. What I came to know further is that one of my jobs in this lifetime is to bring to the attention of healers the existence of Transcendence and to offer them the opportunity of realigning their practice with its pure vibration.

It was in 2005 at a spiritual healing workshop, when listening to someone recounting an experience he had had a couple of times, and quite legitimately basing his workshop on it, that I felt stunned. I was propelled into a state of questioning: What am I doing not talking of my experiences when I have them regularly? Anyone who has reached a state of spiritual knowing feels compelled to speak of it, to tell others what is available to them. I finally understood I had been resisting this deep pressure for years. Friends and family were the only people to benefit from my quiet passion. At the end of the seminar the speaker said there was debate about whether or not it was necessary for the highest awareness to be maintained in individual consciousness before having the right to call oneself enlightened. Many spiritual teachers, he claimed, felt it was not necessary. I understood then that, despite my reservations, I would have to speak out. This feeling was compounded by a later workshop run by someone claiming to be in touch with Avatars. I was again left with the impression that I should speak of my own understanding about the underlying purpose of existence. During the following year, on a trip to Germany, I met two women expressing a desire to know what they called God. I was concerned that they were taking the most difficult route. They were reading self-help books, analyzing their every thought then rereading the books time and again, in the belief that they were reaching states of enlightenment from an analysis of their problems. This was the icing on the cake for me and another push. I was upset that experiences of expanded states of consciousness and the nature of enlightenment were not clearly defined for them. This had resulted in a clouding of their expectations. I was also unhappy that so much energy was being spent on activities which were neither as fast, nor as easy, as the Transcendent teachings that I had been fortunate to find.

The decision to put pen to paper began to unfold slowly. A subsequent realization, after an intense period of self-questioning and change lasting several years, served to show me that I had to accept my experience was not run-of-the-mill and I did sometimes have answers based on my own understanding. But still, even within the TM arena when general questions were raised about the sort of experiences that I had, I did not speak of mine. My natural inclination is to be a hermit. Although I enjoy travel and the city and its attractions I spend much of my time alone, and many hours in meditation. In a multitude of lives in the past I have done this. One life in particular springs to mind. My role in that lifetime was to go out into the world to teach the wisdom of Transcendence and I was given the skills I needed to undertake the work. Instead of fulfilling this duty I shunned it for what I perceived at the time as the security of a life as a hermit. My desire to avoid the reactions of others, a stored response to previous life experiences, had overcome my desire to spread this message. Living in the depth of the forest I was happy because my only duty, as I saw it at the time, was to meditate and develop spiritually. The same behavior has been displayed within this life.

On a few occasions I have shed awareness of my physical form. Once, in the unlikely setting of a busy office, I realized myself in the light-form I had been before I incarnated. I saw Mother Divine at my side, standing beside me emanating her glorious light. I was shown my Divine duty, my work. I did not believe what I was seeing or hearing. I did not think it was possible. A fear predominated that what I was experiencing was my own ego, projected. I have since had to accept this role, knowing that if I refuse my life on the physical plane will be unfulfilled, even though fulfilled inwardly. This sense of my responsibility was brought home to me again during a conversation with someone at a healing center. I was made to look at the people in the room and told that I had to do something to get my wisdom to a wider audience. I was warned that time was not on my side, that other people were "playing at this" and reminded that, with me, it was a vocation. "In any other life you would be a nun," I was told. As I was spoken to I was aware of a timeless wisdom being expressed. I knew this person had spoken to me in this way before; I had previously been guided by him in the physical world and I entered a state of awareness where I experienced knowing him since the beginning of time. From that moment on I began to change my pattern of not reaching out to others. Slowly but surely the hermit began to emerge from the forest.

Since 1999 the infinite in the form of Mother Divine has been my constant inner companion and guide, teaching me about healing, answering my every question. She has taken me beyond apparent boundaries to know her in her quintessential, Absolute Transcendent nature. During this time of learning a level head has been a necessity and a lack of imagination has been a great asset. Nowadays it has developed into my own understanding with no obvious intermediary. The experience of communicating with the Divine is the experience of Divine vibration within inner unending silence and joy. But this journey to Transcendence has been one of determination and persistence. On an inner Transcendent level I have experienced the universe within and heard its original vibration. I live past and present lives simultaneously, without the boundaries of time, know the light of Transcendence and have inhabited a world where objects are moved with the light of thoughts alone. The laws of karma are impossible to fathom with the mind, but there have been visions of the great laws, as if in a giant jigsaw, fitting together and highlighting the order underlying the seemly random events of life. I am familiar with the finer atmosphere in which angels reside, see spirals and shafts of light beaming into rooms and have experienced 360° vision. Sometimes all I see of people in a room is their inner vibration and the vibration they project towards me, be it dark or light. But all these are as nothing compared with the real spiritual experience of Transcendent, Divine union. I know what it is to hold an awareness of my true nature, perceiving even thoughts and emotions as material objects which provide empty fulfillment in comparison with the endless flow of self-fulfilling inner bliss. I understand what it is to be the Transcendent essence of Buddha or Shiva. After being permitted to see Her as she really is, in both Her aspects male and female, knowledge of Mother Divine without physical form finally permeated my consciousness. On a physical level this life has been a life of manifestations, magic and some struggle. Over the last few years I have argued with Her, turned my back on Her for periods of time and have demanded much. But ultimately to know the Divine is to know love. It means also the compulsion to speak of it, to talk of the capacity that we all have within. Inwardly Mother Divine has told me I must tell of the love I hold for Her in my heart, speak of light and my own awakening to show the possibilities. The Transcendence embodied by the Mother is the essence of us all and can be realized by every human being. The states of consciousness available are glorious. To know the Mother completely is to have the wisdom of Transcendent vision and to allow individual ego to merge into Divine.

This journey has led me to believe there is a creative force in the universe which is the foundation, provider and essence of all there is. So powerful, all-embracing and loving is this, the most apt name, for me, is God. Whatever the name given, it is possible to have an intimate relationship with this Transcendent Divine Creator. The experience of this is one of both infinite inner expansion and ecstasy, but above all, it is sacred. Some time ago, walking through the forest surrounding the Iguassu Waterfalls on the border of Argentina and Brazil, marveling at the colors of the exotic birds, I slipped into an expanded state of consciousness. Behind the facade of this scene I saw Mother Divine playing a violin and the whole of creation stream forth as her music. We are all notes in the music of Divine expression but every one of us can choose to change their place in the melody.

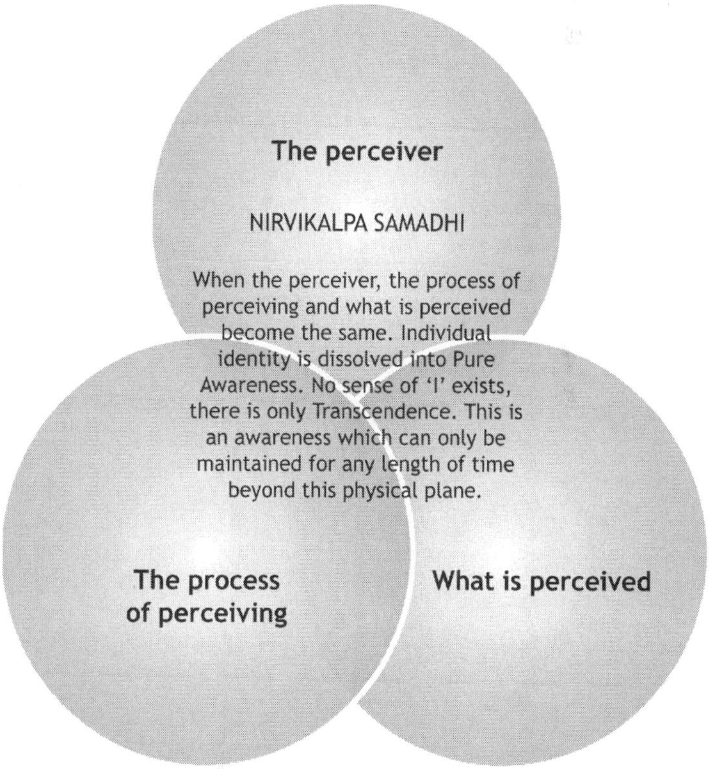

Each individual has a different reality, but there is only one destination, one Truth.

An Evolutionary Structure

3

Transcendent Grace

~ Transcendence ~

The Source of everything is Transcendence, Pure Awareness, unendingly, ecstatically, aware of itself. God is nothing but Transcendent, Pure Awareness. Deep within Transcendence, within the indivisible, lie the seeds for the divisible, the wisdom needed to give rise to a material creation. The Pure Awareness that is Transcendence emanates pure light. This realm of pure light is the place of all wisdom, the home of the laws of creation, freedom of choice and its effects and ramifications (called karma). The created outer reactive light which emerges from it is governed by these laws.

~ The Godhead ~

From silent Transcendence came Transcendence in action, an active Creator with the potential and power, through desire, to express itself. The outward breath of this Creator spiraling outwards gave rise to an expansion of the physical world. This eventually becomes an inward breath, contraction and dissolution of matter. All expression has vibration. All vibration has light and sound and shape (or form). Both the Vedas[1] and the Bible describe this finest vibration as the 'Word'. The Vedas talk about the Word being second to the Lord of Creation, the 'Om'. In the Bible[2/3] it says:

> In the beginning was the Word, and the Word was with God, and the Word was God.

And:

...Let there be light: and there was light.

This vibration of light and sound and form is the most subtle, and from it comes space. Next emerge the properties that make up the physical forms we all know: air, fire, water and earth. This Creator is the nurturing God of all; only through impulses of Divine Transcendence does life exist. Breath is the link between Transcendence and its expression as an individual life.

This is the aspect of Transcendence which is the Godhead, the three faces of God: Creator, Maintainer and Transformer of everything and the essence of male and female vibrations. The Creator of a potentially human individual spark with freedom of choice, enjoyed within the arena of reactive law, the law of cause and effect. Transcendence emanated a vibration from an impulse to express and bestow the possibility for individuals to become fully conscious, that they could come to know and love the Transcendent God. In order for physical matter to become human, this impulse and spark had to exist.

~ Avatars ~

God exists in three ways: Transcendent, Pure Awareness, the Godhead and the Avatar. Avatars are a continuation of the outward breath and an expression of the Creator. They breathe a pure light vibration further into the physical world. All are the one God of Transcendence.

For the purpose of creation to unfold Transcendence must experience itself. This it does when it is lived purely and clearly through the individual spark that becomes human form. When one of the three faces of the Godhead, Creator, Maintainer and Transformer, incarnates into the physical world this becomes the Avatar. Within Transcendence Avatars exist, within what the

Avatar Ramakrishna[4] described as "the fence made of light". Avatars emerge from the resting place of Nirvikalpa Samadhi, a complete merging of their individual consciousness into Transcendence. They separate themselves from this in order to incarnate into a physical form. Their mastery of their senses and body is complete. Even when taking a physical form they are aware of their Divine Transcendent nature and the Transcendence of the world and its inhabitants. When this particular awareness is maintained in the world, it is the less exalted, yet enlightened, awareness of Bhavamukha. Ramakrishna[5] himself adopted this aspect. Incarnation takes place in order to make their presence felt and to dispense their Grace in the world. Avatars are a direct descent and so are Transcendence in human form. They embody and express the essential qualities of knowing Transcendence: joy, love and compassion. Their bodies emit the pure light of a Transcendent vibration which has the potential to purify outer denser vibrations; they can raise the vibration of others. The combination of unconditional love and Transcendence in human form results in a purifying Grace. With their boundless compassion, the sole desire of the Avatar is to alleviate the suffering of humanity. This they do through their darshan, the display of their Self-realized presence. For those individuals who are unable to sustain within themselves a direct relationship with the Godhead, the Avatar is the intermediary. They ensure that Transcendence is the intermediary. They display themselves in the world to show humanity the possibilities, their light illuminates those around them and, if those it touches are willing, its pure vibration transmutes unwanted karma and its associated distress. Grace is the release of individuals from the results of their own desires and creations. Every movement of a Self-realized Avatar is a dispensation of Divine Grace. Every footstep, thought, touch or look expresses and releases a pure light vibration into the arena of form, which is the physical world. Even their name emanates a Transcendent vibration. They help to raise the awareness of individuals and the world. Buddha[6] translated by Thomas Byrom said:

> The followers of the awakened
> Awake
> And day and night they watch
> And meditate upon their master.

Like a machine designed to attract and destroy flies Avatars attract spiritual seekers and burn the roots of their karma in a way that is theirs alone. The Avatar speeds up the process of spiritual evolution. Without the Avatar this world would be a desert: physically, emotionally, morally and spiritually. It is only because of their Transcendent Grace showered onto creation that spiritual progress and the march towards greater comfort and happiness is assured. With their co-operation other individuals will become aware of this process.

The individual consciousness of the Avatar is beyond suffering. It is the identification and empathy they adopt which means they are compassionate about others' pain. Avatars undergo the same stresses as everyone else but know their difference. They show the rest of humanity that suffering can be transcended. Avatars hold no past attachments. Their only karma is their desire to help humanity. But Avatars, like the rest of humanity, work within the framework of denser, reactive, physical light and its essence of free will, choice, self-responsibility, effects and ramifications. Their incarnation has consequences. It offers the choice of spirituality. The greatness of Avatars is that, although they could, they do not interfere with the free will and choices of others. Jesus could have prevented his physical suffering but did not. He did not have to die on the cross but allowed this event to take place as the choice made by humanity. Avatars incarnate simply to offer their purifying Grace, to absorb and transmute karma and accelerate spiritual awareness. In order to do this they are prepared to suffer physically. Jesus's suffering on the cross was the transmutation of karma, through his physical form, for the salvation of others. Being ensconced in a constricted physical form is their suffering; at the same time they are quite beyond it, the veil they use to separate themselves from their true nature being lifted with ease. Only one living with Transcendent Awareness can dispense transmuting Grace through their physical being.

Avatars do not spiritually evolve in our sense of the word but they become more adept at incorporating their special skills into their physical selves. They progress in expressing the evolutionary impulses of the Divine. Avatars will respond to the suffering of the collective and the needs of the day, displaying their wisdom in a style which relates to a particular audience. The existence and behavior of the Avatars who incarnate, the versatility of their Transcendent teachings and the cognition of humanity, will be in accordance with the collective spiritual consciousness of the time. Avatars will choose their individual manner. They may adopt a detached, ecstatic manner, living in total inner bliss unaffected by the world, or they may inhabit a compassionate, empathetic consciousness. Ramakrishna displayed the detached manner of the Avatar when he was said to be ecstatic about the death of his nephew. He even danced around the body. The following day this manner changed to one that embodied empathy for the pain experienced by unenlightened friends and relatives. The empathetic manner is the usual one adopted by Avatars in the form of Mother Divine; it is Mother Divine who identifies with the suffering of humankind.

Avatars have a close connection to the evolutionary impulse of the Godhead and they express it clearly. The power of this was displayed by the miracles Jesus performed, the raising of Lazarus being the most spectacular. When he was told of Lazarus's death he was aware of an opportunity. Breath is the life-thread which connects us to consciousness. There are two qualities to the life-thread: the karmic quality and the life-force quality. The karmic quality is thoroughly used when the individual has had access to the potential karmic experience they have incarnated with. When the body is unable to accommodate any more, both qualities are severed. Breath is withdrawn from the physical body and it decays. When Lazarus died Jesus was able to reconnect the life-thread of a future incarnation. This could only take place with the sanction of the higher aspect of the Godhead and certain conditions had to be met. The body of Lazarus, despite its obvious decay, must not have deteriorated beyond a specified degree. In addition, Lazarus's physical form, culture and personality needed to be suitable to accommodate his future karma which was embedded within his new life-thread. It would also be possible, but only in defined situations and with the approval of the Godhead, for the Avatar to create a new, potentially human, individual spark.

A child brought up by wolves imitates their behavior and comes to believe that he is the same as the wolf. He is unaware of his human potential. Similarly, the reality of humanity's Divine nature cannot be realized until one who knows his or her Divine status displays it. In the dense physical world of reactive light, spiritual wisdom and Grace filter through the pure physical system of the Avatar. Knowing their own true nature, Avatars help to awaken in others an awareness of their own, hidden Transcendence. Avatars do this by teaching, and by emanating a pure, transmuting, Transcendent light vibration in a way that is theirs alone.

~ Teachers ~

After Avatars come teachers. The teachers lead others towards the Avatars. Teachers have a special relationship with the Avatar, a connecting light from Avatar to teacher, forged at the beginning of time. Teachers assist Avatars in spreading their teaching in the world; they help humankind to recognize and accept it. The link of light the teachers have with the Avatar allows them to assimilate and disseminate pure light and wisdom on their behalf. In the way that Jesus bestowed spiritual power to his disciples the Avatar does this to the teachers. These teachers too delay their own merging into Nirvikalpa Samadhi for the benefit of humanity. They also bring the Grace of the Avatar, to a lesser degree with their own light, and in the blessing of liberation from suffering ensconced within their Transcendent teachings. The teachers ensure that Transcendent techniques are available to the rest of humanity, knowing it is more likely to adopt a systematic practice than a devotional one towards the Avatar. There are recluse teachers and householder teachers. Householder is a word to refer to individuals who live everyday family lives, unlike the teachers who are monks and hermits and who appeal less to those with jobs and family responsibilities. The householder teachers appeal more to humanity because they live similar lives. In this world these teachers realize their Divine Transcendent nature quickly, desiring and accepting with inner willingness the teaching and Grace of the Avatar. The impulses and wisdom for this rapid spiritual evolution in the teachers is established within them, quickening their desire for growth in Transcendent Awareness. It is from their own experience of enlightened states of consciousness that they teach. As Buddha[7] said:

> In this world the wise man
> Becomes himself a light,
> Pure, shining, free.

Anyone who realizes their true nature will have the capacity to disseminate Grace.

~ Transcendent Teachings ~

Transcendent teachings are teachings and techniques which directly access a pure Transcendent light vibration. Using these when healing or meditating ensures that attention is drawn straight towards Transcendence; there is no intermediary when these teachings are employed other than Transcendence itself. The outcome is faster spiritual development. Grace is disseminated through direct contact with Transcendence, purifying an individual's physical vibration and releasing them from their unwanted karma. Transcendent techniques are the offer to humanity of an easy and quick route to the inner liberation of enlightenment.

~ Celestial Helpers ~

The Grace of the Avatar and the Transcendent teachings could not be disseminated further without the assistance of the celestial helpers. They are indispensible for the progression of spiritual awareness in the world. The celestial helpers are close to the teachers. They recognize the teachers, the value of Transcendent teachings and the Avatars. They help both. The celestial helpers who adopt a householder nature are closer to the rest of humanity than the teachers and will spread their teaching to an even greater extent. Their householder nature ensures they understand and identify even more closely with the rest of humanity. Others will listen to them readily because of their similarity, unlike the recluse teachers and Avatars who do not have the same type of responsibilities. The celestial helpers relate to both the teachers and the population at large and so are a vital link between the teachers, the teaching and the rest of humanity.

This is the spiritual hierarchy. There has always been a spiritual hierarchy, there always will be. Its seeds are a part of the physical structure of the universe, existing since the beginning of creation. This hierarchical structure prevails to help humanity. It expresses an impulse from the totality that is Transcendence and it is this expression which assists in the unfolding of Transcendent Awareness in humanity. The potential is for all individuals to become aware of Transcendence, the foundation of themselves and the world and so become Self-realized. Individual awareness can reflect Pure Awareness. Eventually it is possible for everyone to merge totally with Transcendence, into Nirvikalpa Samadhi. All humans have the capacity to reach Divine status and know the Avataristic realm. All who do receive Grace. They acknowledge the Avatar as a Divine descent.

Only from Transcendence comes Grace, this alone must be the intermediary.

4

Grace Cascading

There is a steadfast satellite of love in the universe. From an impulse to experience itself, Transcendence brought into existence a hierarchical structure which would light the pathway towards it for everyone. In the outward breath of the Transcendent Creator were the impulses needed to realize a wonderful dream, the seeds for a hierarchical structure that has come and gone, as an element of previous creations, and will come and go again. Between creation – activity and expansion, and dissolution, inactivity and contraction – the memory of the structure is retained waiting to be reinvigorated. The creation of diversity fuelled by wisdom, love, compassion and a conscious desire for joyful experience. All the Avatars, teachers and celestial helpers were visible to humanity at the beginning of creation and could be again at the end of this cycle of experience. In the form of light I see this created hierarchy surrounded by a river with a bridge linking them to the rest of humanity. In this lifetime an Avatar, incarnated into the physical form of Mother Divine, told me that the bridge I have seen is "the bridge of love". The purpose is for all individuals to have an opportunity to grow in awareness and merge their individual consciousness with Transcendence. In achieving this they will consciously inhabit their finest physical body of pure light and enjoy and express their own special talents. It is thanks to the Avatars, teachers and helpers that Grace cascades into the world. Without this there would be stagnation and little spiritual progress. Grace and wisdom cascade down the structure via two routes: systematic Transcendent teachings, and the compassionate response to suffering bestowed on humanity by the Avatar.

Woven into the individuality of the spiritual hierarchy are their roles and spiritual wisdom. Between the Avatars and the bridge are the teachers: recluse and householder. Next come the celestial helpers whose position between the teachers and proximity to the rest of the population is significant. They stand by the bridge as a link, encouraging the rest of humanity to move towards Transcendence and salvation. This is a paradise that none had to leave. We, every one of us, are Transcendence in our quintessential nature. At the beginning of creation all humanity had to do was to take a short walk across the bridge, towards the integration of Transcendence which is enlightenment. They could have enjoyed its fulfillment and from there merged totally into the goal of Nirvikalpa Samadhi, life in its totality of endless ecstasy: a life so complete that none would wish to leave other than to help others also realize their own infinite nature.

Living in the first light-body humanity was graced with the capability of bringing into being physical form from thought. Life was lived in an arena of instant gratification, created from desire through the mind. In this way the world was formed. But individuals were enticed by it. Instead of walking towards enlightenment humankind turned away, entranced and immersed in density. So good was everything at the beginning of creation it was difficult to believe that greater peace and happiness was possible and there was little impetus to become Self-realized. As Buddha[1] in Thomas Byrom's translation said:

Few cross over the river.
Most are stranded on this side.
On the riverbank they run up and down.
But the wise man, following the way,
Crosses over, beyond the reach of death.

Humanity became attracted to its creations and eventually distracted by them. Distraction became clutching, then attachment and identification. It was overshadowed by its fascination with the world, to the point where awareness of its Transcendence was lost. Humankind became identified instead with the form it had created. Into this arena of physical reactive light, emanating from Divine Transcendence but jointly formed, it sank. The possibility of Transcendence was forgotten. So dense was the creation that individual human existence could only appear in the world through a material evolution from mineral to vegetable to animal towards the raised evolutionary form of human. Becoming human was due to the special God-given individual spark, finally finding through the evolution of matter its physical expression in the world. Choice and being conscious of making choices reflects evolution. It came from the development of mind, but with choice came the abandonment of instinct and the gaining of responsibility.

For every desire there is a physical reflection. Our present world is a reflection of the collective spiritual consciousness and desires of its inhabitants. It is extreme diversity, from hot to cold, wet to dry, dark to light, suffering to joy, love to hate, living and dying. The life humanity leads is the web it weaves. But despite the dense nature of the world, the Transcendent indivisible from which the divisible came is its true reality. Although the world has the appearance of diversity, it is a facade. Within each individual is eternity waiting to be fully experienced; living it will illuminate the outer edges of creation. Humanity's underlying misery is due to this missing experience. This lack of awareness is the source of all its suffering. The denser the vibrations of light which make up the world, the greater the potential for individual and collective suffering. In the environment of physical matter restlessness predominates. Sri Aurobindo[2] quoted by Robert A. McDermott said:

> But man cannot rest permanently until he reaches some highest good. He is the greatest of living beings because he is the most discontented, because he feels most the pressure of limitations.

Life in the dense physical reactive light of this world is the perfect impetus. The undercurrent caused by this is the discomfort and unhappiness which nudges humanity to search for a better existence. But it was never necessary to suffer; it is not necessary now. In merging with totality, all will realize that the world and its diversity is nothing but the unity of Transcendence.

As humanity turned towards form, Avatars crossed the bridge willingly. They separated themselves from their own merging in Nirvikalpa Samadhi. For the benefit of humankind they took a human body as an act of Grace. By being pure instruments of Divine Transcendent Awareness, they absorb and eradicate the suffering of humanity. The further away from Transcendence, the less power is commanded and the more entrenched in reactive light individuals are. This is what the structure shows us. It is its great teaching. The purity of the Avatar, their liberated consciousness and physical being which emanates Grace ensure they never become entranced and entrenched in reactive light and its ramifications. The teachers also delayed their own individual merging and fulfillment. Along with the celestial helpers, knowingly and willingly, they also reached out towards humanity. From their love, compassion, and desire to teach how to reach the Transcendent home, these teachers and helpers created their own physical form of reactive light, understanding as they did so that they would be living in the arena of reactive, karmic law of cause and effect. So those who could have remained stepped forward, inspired and directed by love and became caught up in the drama of form. Life after life of separation was lived as their service to humanity. The Avatars, teachers and helpers continue to inform about the possibility of a direct relationship with the Divine. Still they teach that a journey over the bridge in the opposite direction, away from the diversity of the physical world towards Transcendence, would prevent suffering.

The structure of the world also emanated from Transcendence, each country containing the seeds of its individual attributes. Created within the same moment was India, the holder of wisdom, the home of the Avatars and Transcendent teachings. Transcendent wisdom spreads from here. This wisdom is preserved in the Vedas[3], the sacred texts of India, and recognized as guidance for all with its Sanskrit descriptions of many different states of consciousness. In the beginning the essential positive qualities of all countries in their pure form were created. Alongside India as the guardian of spiritual wisdom are the attributes, often related to the British, of a love of justice and tolerance. America exhibits an enthusiastic and innovative nature and Scandinavians self-containment. There is the kindness and courtesy of Cambodia and the honoring and discipline associated with the Japanese. Then there is the vibration of Africa which touches the heart. The shape and forms of these countries have changed and evolved with the flow of time, as has the display of their qualities. But the harmonious working together of all nations could be the reality, each country excelling in, and radiating, their own special features.

Although we are only part of the way through a murky age, small peaks of higher perception are appearing within the darkness. Presently there are few who have reached a state of spiritual discernment. Today the surge of evolution means that through the use of particularly advanced and versatile Transcendent techniques, a transmuting vibration can awaken further the Divine Transcendence of the world. This has become a possibility in spite of the fact that people using them have yet to reach Self-realized status. It will occur, however, only through the use of techniques which are pure and accurately taught. An increase in this human capability will facilitate real spiritual transformation in the world, where, even when enlightenment is not the norm, the highest vibration of light is established in its creations of time and form. It will be a melding of inner Transcendent light and outer, reflected reactive light on a scale that has never happened before. Each Avatar comes with a teaching and healing response relevant to the time, so it is with Transcendent teachings that come to public consciousness. These teachings have always existed but not been utilized, only coming to public consciousness when the awareness of humanity develops to the point where it is able to perceive and appreciate them. Only through the intermediary of Transcendence will this work proceed with speed.

The purpose of human creation is for everyone to realize their Transcendence. Jesus[4] told us:

> ...the kingdom of God is within you.

But as humans we have choice and until we choose this Divine status reincarnation and distress will continue. Only when an individual reaches the supreme state of spiritual evolution comes the Self-realization which is the unity of Transcendence. The reality is that the one who experiences, the object which is experienced, and the means of connecting the two are the same. They are all Transcendence and gaining this individual consciousness is a bestowal of Grace from the Avatar. There is only one effective and fast route to this experience; it is the direct one. There is only one truly helpful intermediary and it takes two forms: Transcendence in the form of the true Avatar, and Transcendent teachings. Any other intermediary may become a distraction, and an eventual clutching, resulting in an attachment and identification with its form. The crossing of the Avatars, teachers and helpers was nothing more than their desire converted to thought. In reality they have never moved. Like a waterfall the structure ensures Transcendent wisdom cascades downwards towards humanity.

The form of this world is as it should be, not because it is the way it should be, but because it is the way we have shaped it. It is our mirror.

Beyond Angels ~ Towards Transcendence

5

A Wisdom Lost

The morning of February 6th 2008 was the day after the death of Maharishi Mahesh Yogi. Maharishi had brought the ancient teaching of Transcendental Meditation™ out of India to the attention of those in the West. In my opinion he was one of the greatest teachers of the spiritual hierarchy. In the commentaries I heard on his passing very little of Maharishi's true mission came to light. Much focused on The Beatles, much on the wealth of his charity. He was made fun of. This seemed to me indicative of the state of the collective spiritual consciousness of our time; news of the death of the man who had been responsible for a great transformation in human consciousness was not deemed worthy of a serious airing. Maharishi came from the Shankaracharya tradition and he introduced the wisdom of the Vedas[1], which previously had been the wisdom of recluses, to householders in the West. For the first time, on a large scale, people who had previously thought that meditation was the sole preserve of hermits could access its benefits. Suddenly parents, business people, the elderly and children were able to learn this profound meditation. Getting up at 4.00am to meditate is the routine of a monk, not a householder who more often than not has family responsibilities. Maharishi created the possibility of enlightenment for those whose responsibilities and karma was not to lock themselves away in isolation, but to remain involved in worldly activity. For me it was no coincidence that he was born into the Kshatriya caste, traditionally understood as the warrior or protector caste. It is this caste which has been associated with the protection of Vedic wisdom. I believe that Maharishi's mission was the creation of a transcendental 'light army' here on earth. He strategically placed this 'army' of meditators to effectively establish, maintain and increase a pure vibration of light in the world. In so doing he was assisting a smoother transition from the present dark age into a future lighter one and supporting an upsurge, albeit small, of Transcendent Awareness into the individual consciousness of many. Ageless wisdom was incorporated within the fullness of his teaching. But judging by the media coverage, the current state of collective world consciousness has little understanding of the existence of Transcendence and its inherent wisdom as the creative, nurturing and sustaining force of the universe. The true measure of the man whose individual state of consciousness embodied this wisdom, sadly, appeared lost to the general public.

Maharishi taught me profound truths directly. Alongside these were others which were also fully understood through my own experience:

- Firstly: I realized the beautiful truth of Transcendence, that changing my consciousness changed my world. The more I meditated the more my behavior spontaneously changed. I learned through my immersion in Transcen-dence that my life was a reflection of my consciousness.

- Secondly: it is possible for action to be instigated from an impulse which is spiritually evolutionary or from one that is not, (although on the surface the result of these actions may appear to be the same). The implication of this is that the latter is less supportive for the expansion of an individual's awareness. I noted many times that differences in the vibration of an impulse, even when unconscious, had an impact on the spirituality of the action. The amount of support for spiritual growth varied according to this impulse (I discuss in Chapter 8 the varying wisdoms in different vibrations of light).

- Thirdly: my time in the healing / New-Age arena placed me in an environment where I was able to see at close quarters the quality of the therapies that were on offer. Most of them lacked the Transcendent approach, which I understood from my very first year of meditating, so spontaneously changed life and behavior, permanently, easily and from within.

- Finally: that understanding of the world depends on an individual's spiritual awareness. Being close to both skeptics and experienced meditators helped me see clearly that wisdom and the discernment that emanates from it is determined by this one criterion. Just as the skeptic only sees the motives of self-interest, the gullible sees nothing of the hidden motives. Neither can see the other's viewpoint. The perception of both the skeptic and the gullible is filtered and understood through individual awareness. The same is true for those who consider themselves to be spiritual. Being close to those who believed themselves to be spiritually aware, yet were not enlightened, was also a teaching for me. It highlighted clearly how misunderstood words like 'presence', 'now' and 'mindfulness' were when used by one who had no full experience of their Transcendent quality. In other words, understanding about the world is determined by awareness and an unenlightened consciousness (either in one open to spiritual teaching or in the skeptic) can never perceive with the clarity or understanding of one who has gained enlightenment. There is therefore always a gap of misunderstanding between an enlightened teaching and its reception. Like the nightmare that feels real and is only revealed as a dream on waking, whatever the state of spiritual awareness and subsequent understanding about the world a person has, it appears real and full to them at

> the time they experience it. Moving into the most expanded state of awareness, being awake to the fullness of Transcendence, means that the cloudiness of past states of consciousness is appreciated. Only from the fully expanded perspective of enlightenment can an assessment of what is seen be full, thoroughly penetrating and wise. Judgments then cease to be based on partial understandings but gain the objective, unmoving, stable, eternal basis of Transcendence. Action, which is then based on the greatest spiritual discernment, becomes spontaneously the most appropriate for the spiritual well-being of all concerned. The vision of any individual's consciousness when not aware of Transcendence is obscured by their own denser vibrations. In my experience, many events I thought I understood fully the first time round, I later came to see with greater lucidity. Many are the times that I believed I had understood enlightened teaching only to understand more deeply at a future point. It eventually became clear to me that it was only possible to truly understand enlightenment when in a state of enlightenment.

These teachings were proffered by many previous Self-realized Masters who said exactly the same thing: the Transcendence incorporated within an individual's awareness will relate to the clarity of that individual's understanding. Their action will be based on that understanding. Their action has consequences and these will affect the quality of life.

Alongside working tirelessly to maintain the purity of TM, Maharishi ensured the safe keeping of Vedic teaching in India, from where the technique originated in its uncorrupted form. In the Vedic tradition wisdom is handed down from one enlightened custodian to another. This is how the quality of its techniques is maintained, by ensuring that only those who are Self-realized, and so fully able to understand its wisdom, are its keepers. The word 'veda' comes from the Sanskrit root *'vid'* translated as 'to know'. The body of writing included under the umbrella name of the Veda is thought to be the most ancient written record of 'life-wisdom' and is usually passed on orally. Generally believed, although not certain, to have appeared in north-west India via the Aryan civilization, it is said to contain truths that were cognized at the beginning of time by the enlightened. The Veda is still the collective name for the sacred texts of Hinduism, the most famous of which are the 'Rig Veda' and the 'Upanishads'. The epic Indian work the 'Mahabharata' was finished later, around the time of the start of the Christian era, although its origins appear to predate this as its teaching is an embodiment of Vedic wisdom. The Mahabharata contains within it a story called the 'Bhagavad-Gita'. The wisdom in these chapters is thought to have been compiled millennia ago by the sage Vyasa. The Vedas speak about the Transcendent reality which lies beneath the diversity of the physical world of form and of how it is possible to live both sides of life, infinite Transcendent Pure Awareness alongside material life. The Bhagavad-Gita teaches us that when only the physical side of life is lived and when an awareness of Transcendence is forgotten, suffering ensues. This can happen on both an individual and a collective level. The Bhagavad-Gita tells the well-known story of how 5,000 years ago the Avatar Krishna incarnated to restore this spiritual wisdom to humankind. The embodiment of Transcendence in the personality of Krishna came to relieve humanity's pain. He dispensed Grace for those who had direct contact with Him and His teaching. The story goes that Divine Grace was received by Arjuna when, on the battlefield, the person he had previously believed to be only his friend (Krishna) showed himself to be an Avatar, the Godhead in human form. Krishna bestowed on Arjuna the ultimate Grace of enlightenment. He taught Arjuna that Transcendence was the foundation and impulse for everything in existence. Arjuna was told that over time the knowledge that awareness of Transcendence as the basis for a better life gets forgotten. And, when this happens another Divine personality will come to revive it.

When suffering predominates the cries and prayers are heard by the hierarchy. The response that the Bhagavad-Gita speaks of comes in the form of the Avatars who incarnate to dispense Grace through their Transcendent presence. Their spiritually evolutionary impulses help humankind to see the way to release themselves from their distress. With them will come teachers who teach effective Transcendent techniques which also embody this blessing. Celestial helpers will also appear to facilitate the process. Incorporating Transcendence into human awareness is a release from individual and collective adversity and the purpose of human incarnation. A compassionate God always responds to the suffering of humanity with Grace. Since the beginning of creation knowledge of Transcendence has come and gone and many Avatars have made a direct descent in order to disseminate their wisdom. Not only Krishna, Ramakrishna, Buddha and Jesus, but many forms of Mother Divine have entered this realm, to teach through different means the value of incorporating Transcendence into individual awareness.

This call by all the past Masters for a Transcendent approach to life is a 'consciousness-first' approach. It is my belief that a consciousness-first wisdom needs to be applied to the New-Age movement's healing and meditation practices. Present day New-Age teaching is more often than not built on the tenet of misunderstood 'truth': that, in order to develop spiritually, what is in fact the result of development (behavior) has first to be addressed. But, behavior is a *reflection* of spiritual awareness. Harmonious activity is mistaken as the means to achieve enlightenment rather than being seen as its outcome. The nub of this small book is to suggest to the New-Age movement the opposite: first expand individual consciousness then undesired behavior will spontaneously improve.

Turbulent Impressions

Some years ago, waiting to take off from San Francisco airport, the pilot informed us the wind at Heathrow was "manageable". The flight over the Atlantic was perfectly smooth until we reached London where we began to feel we were on a fairground ride. To add to our discomfort we had to circle Heathrow for about 20 minutes before being given permission to land. Coming in to land we had almost touched the tarmac when the landing was abruptly aborted and we took off again. We circled the airport for another 20 minutes. This time passengers were fearful and some were physically sick. The pilot eventually informed us that he had aborted the landing as there had been a plane on the runway. My partner said there was anxiety in his voice and he thought the strong gusts of wind had been a factor.

For some time afterwards when flying, each time the plane approached the runway I prepared myself in case we had to abandon the landing. The impression left by the event had remained. I had stored the emotions and stress from the experience of the first flight in my memory. A similar scenario, another landing, reinvoked them and their behavioral responses. I was holding a painful pattern. This was a minor happening for me, its effects were not long lasting or painful compared with others. Nevertheless, it is quite usual that residual emotions from a more painful past situation are triggered by similar, yet often seemingly minor, events. These hidden emotions are often projected, pinned onto apparently unrelated people and events, and their objects are made the scapegoats.

In the absence of the Divine, fear has been the mechanism through which individuals have kept safe, but with inner Divine guidance this changes. The present-day healing solution would be to re-examine the fear and its trigger and attempt to alter the response. This is hard work. What is needed is a method which expands consciousness to the point where an individual is liberated, insulated from the provocation of the trigger. In comparison, this sort of healing is easy and soothing and does not run the risk of compounding the effect of the memories; always a possibility when they are brought into conscious awareness.

Patanjali[2], translated by Alistair Shearer, said:

> The impressions of past action, stored deep in the mind, are the seeds of desire.
> They ripen into action in seen and unseen ways – if not in this life, then in a future one.

The essence of New-Age therapies' approach to physical problems is the analysis of behavior, firstly, from an intellectual starting point, later attempting to alter it and eventually hoping to instigate more positive activity. There is nothing inherently wrong with understanding responses to events intellectually. However, there is an infinite difference between having a limited intellectual awareness of habits and difficulties and gaining a boundless Transcendent Awareness which liberates an individual from the distress. The New-Age movement is offering outer-to-inner procedures, rather than a consciousness-first, which is inner-to-outer. There are a number of difficulties with an outer-to-inner methodology:

- It is utilizing the same intermediary which created the problem in the first place: the mind. Furthermore, it is the faculty of a mind absorbed in, and attached to, emotions, memories and unconscious motives which cast shadows over Pure Awareness. The mind and body are the reflectors of an individual's state of spiritual awareness: without expanding awareness significantly the mind will not be expanded. Latent impressions from the past (in the form of previous beliefs and emotions) will not be dissolved, and so a release from holding onto patterns of responses not realized. An intellectual dissection of the mind is not its release. Without the full force of Transcendence the mind and body may begin to display similar patterns again, possibly in a different way by presenting different behavior. This type of analysis lacks the liberating, transmuting Grace that an inner-to-outer, consciousness-first approach brings. A Transcendent intermediary ensures a direct experience of Transcendence; it is this which will release an individual's emotional clinging and subsequent responses. Unwanted behavior has to be replaced by something more positive. It has to be substituted by the pure and fulfilling vibration of Transcendent unconditional love.

- An outer-to-inner therapeutic practice, rather than a consciousness-first method, is often offered by New-Age therapists as spiritually developmental. In other words, if a certain behavior is encouraged or a problem fades in their client, it is undoubtedly the result of an expansion of their client's awareness. This is not necessarily the case. Techniques are only spiritually enhancing if the mind and body are infused with Transcendence, so replacing a denser vibration with a pure one. Only this will melt the unwanted emotions and attachments which instigated the undesired conduct.

- An outer-to-inner attempt to rectify unwanted habits is an attempt to 'work back' through the human physiology and its past. This is time-consuming, tedious and often emotionally painful. It is impossible to retrace every step. The effortless experience of Transcendence, its vibration which reverberates throughout the body and mind and purifies them without intellectual investigation, is fast and joyful. Improvements in behavior will automatically come from this.

The serial dieter who yo-yos between fasting and bingeing will never lose their painful attachment to food, which can manifest itself in many ways, until the unconscious, denser impulses which incite them to seek solace in food, are replaced by a purer vibration. Not by analyzing these impulses will they be easily dealt with. They must be exposed to the Grace of a Transcendent vibration which will dissolve them into a higher vibration and expand awareness, a 'decluttering' from Source. Just as dusting the leaves of a plant does not make it healthy, it needs inner nourishment, so merely polishing our behavior cannot supply us with the inner support needed for permanent growth. This simple truth applies to all those who are attempting to heal themselves and / or others. I do not want here to dismiss the New-Age movement completely; I have no wish to imply that investigating only the results of action is inevitably unhelpful but it is by no means necessary. The binge eater may well wish to understand their eating disorder on an intellectual level. Nevertheless, a change in behavior which creates for them a better physical reality, without a corresponding incorporation of Transcendence, may only be a temporary change. At best it creates a more comfortable life from which to attempt to expand consciousness; the alleviation of any problem which results may make that process temporarily easier. At worst, it may establish complacency and an environment which ceases to nudge the perceiver towards true change. If the impulses from subconscious motives and emotions are not dissolved they will resurface. To truly understand habits and attachments they need to be understood from a perspective which knows Transcendence fully. From such a spiritually developed vision they are of little interest as they will have been transcended.

I am proposing that therapists and seekers who are a part of the New-Age movement could achieve more spiritually if they reassess their practices and begin to incorporate faster, more effective techniques. The inner well-being and fulfillment this engenders would promote more physical healing. All healers who do not use spiritually expanding techniques would benefit from being aware of the limitations of their practice. Much New-Age healing focuses on the investigation and correction of what has gone before. Retracing steps and reliving pain is distressing: it is neither necessary nor feasible to go back to where we have been to heal it. In fact, a friend of mine once claimed that her panic attacks were made worse by doing just this. Instead, the solution to a life as free from distress as possible is to introduce Grace. This is available in the two forms I have mentioned previously.

- First: in the form of techniques which give *direct* access to Transcendence, making Transcendence the intermediary to healing. These can be easily added to, or replace, present practices.

- Second: by receiving the blessing of the true Avatar. Visiting them, experiencing their presence and being inwardly open to receiving Grace.

Physical healing and spiritual expansion can be quick and full through one action alone: immersion in Transcendence and integrating it into individual awareness. In using both avenues the fastest progress possible will be made: this involves the combining of the precision of a system with dedication towards the Avatar. All healers need to include a Transcendent consciousness-first approach in their practice, not only for the benefit of their clients, but for their own spiritual well-being.

There is only one lesson, to realize the Divine within. All other understanding comes from this.

6

Fledgling Flight

I remember incarnating with a thought, a part of which was that within this lifetime I would express what I knew. It was the same thought that instigated my first incarnation. I am here now, doing this, suggesting that those who make up the New-Age movement look again at their practices with a view to incorporating within them the pure, unadulterated light of Transcendence, thus creating 'consciousness-first' practices. We have seen the New-Age investigate its past lives and traumas and we have heard about the endless lessons we are here to learn. So dominant and so much a part of the language is this now that even those in the public eye, in accountable positions, consider the promise of 'learning lessons' to be an acceptable response to any lack of skill or responsibility. There is, however, only one lesson for everyone to learn: Self-realization.

I had not understood how difficult it was for baby birds to learn to fly until, over the space of a few days, I watched a young pigeon take its first tentative flights. It did not come easily. At first the small bird refused to try despite the presence of what seemed to be encouraging and despairing parents. After a few days of flight practice it still struggled to retain its balance, landing on a branch but then swinging backwards and forwards in seesaw motion, in a way which made me hold my breath and will it to achieve stability. To me the recent upsurge in New-Age thinking could be likened to the youthful pigeon's fledgling flight. The current teaching of the New-Age movement is a reflection of the spiritual consciousness of the age. It has reached an understanding that there is something over and above what is taken for granted in the minutiae of everyday life. It expresses a greater awareness of energy and its effects, how humanity has the ability to manipulate change, even if temporarily, by altering the patterns of its thoughts. But in its frantic reaching for to the branches of the tree of truth, this fledgling flight of the New-Age movement is fraught with as many obstacles as the baby pigeon's. was. It is precariously perched, unsteady, without the discrimination that comes from experience, and is therefore extremely vulnerable. The New-Age movement's often-used refrain – that individual incorporation of the infinite is achievable, coupled with its lack of knowledge and drive related to reaching this awareness – has ensured this refrain has become its misleading mantra.

When I first began to meditate in 1973 my family was highly anxious, believing I was getting involved in some secret brain-washing sect which would draw me away from them. In those days I did not often tell people that I meditated, only in private situations, and only when the basis of the conversation was relaxation and general well-being. Now my mother also practices meditation and I have been told that including it as a pastime on a CV is advantageous as it is essential that people now record what steps they take to relieve tension. These days meditation is seen as an acceptable method of stress release. I can now also talk more openly about my practice in terms of its self-developmental capacity. Much has changed for the better. But with the growth and establishment of 'a voice' in the shape of the New-Age movement, around me I also find a marketplace full of sensationalism. There is a smorgasbord of therapies (all of which claim to be spiritual) and a plethora of gurus offering the prize of perfect physical or emotional health in exchange for following their teachings. Reiki 'masters' abound, past-life 'regressers' are in full swing and, in the eyes of many, guidance is always deemed worthy. The spiritual status of the expert is rarely questioned. Referring to this current climate

Robert A. McDermott[1] says:

> ...this is a time in our society when claimants to privileged spiritual status and multitudes of uncritical disciples continue to proliferate, when self-proclaimed avatars and genuine gurus are being divinized by zealous disciples...

It seems that the New-Age, too quickly, adds to its multifarious teachings without the necessary discernment. The result is therapies which have only the depth of investigating the impure, reactive light of physical form, the outer light of body, mind and emotions, have come to be seen as suitable means to reach the pure light of Transcendence. As in the example of the yo-yo dieter who tries to control their unwanted habits, behavior which actually *reflects* spiritual development is again being seen as the primary route to achieving it.

I recently went with friends to a New-Age exhibition. The first speaker we saw presented herself and her subject beautifully and the topic raised my interest. She spoke passionately about her experience with meditation and the possibility of a direct communion with the Divine. Her first taste of this had changed her life. At events like these it is rare to hear people talk who have clearly had a truly Divine experience, but at the end of the talk my heart sank. What she was teaching was not a method which offered the same direct connection to Transcendence that she herself had experienced. She taught what I felt to be a disturbing visualization technique; inviting participants to not only put their feet into the ground in the form of 'roots', but to also take their awareness down into the soil. This was not a releasing, enlightening technique but one which felt restricted and potentially created a link to the dense, reactive, physical light of the earth. This is a connection that seekers, particularly those who are sensitive to vibration, would be well advised not to make (this is illustrated further in Chapter 7). She then went on to say that she was selling angel meditation CDs for people to use for their meditation. I asked her why, when she had spoken so engagingly and obviously from the heart about the possibility of a direct experience, she did not teach an unobstructed means to it rather than place in the way an angelic intermediary. The answer was that some people could not make a direct connection and so she had created this "stepping stone" for them. "To sell her CDs" was my friend's suggestion. My heart had expanded when I heard her describe her own experience but it contracted when I saw what she was teaching. My belief that what we understand is dependent on the depth, or limitation, of our awareness comes to the fore every time I hear about this sort of practice. The speaker, despite her own inner knowledge, was clearly not teaching from an enlightened state of awareness. I question whether it was helpful to suggest that others could not make the same connection, albeit temporary, that she herself had made. Placing an intermediary that is not total Transcendence between someone and their own true reality, even if that intermediary is from the angelic realm, runs the risk of a clutching at, and eventually an attachment to, its form. What people see of angels in their practice will depend on the expansiveness of their awareness. Intention is involved and although their intention may be to meditate on angels in order to go beyond them to find the Transcendent God, it is feasible that the meditator may not have this wish. Furthermore, that wish may be diverted.

Many wish to meet beings within the angelic realm but this is more helpfully done as an adjunct to a Transcendent practice. One which directly takes awareness beyond the angelic realm to the Transcendent Source from which they come. Angels are a part of the phenomena of material life, albeit a finer aspect. Angels teach and help, but it is Transcendence which transmutes and releases from the non-evolutionary, and often hidden, impulses that drive humans. Angels are beautiful, breathtaking; the vibration they reside in is charming, becoming more rarefied in the higher angelic realms. Nevertheless it is an arena which is still a part of material life and is a potential distraction. It is perfectly possible to become entranced by it. Like the paradise that could have remained our base (mentioned in Chapter 4) the angelic realm is almost too beautiful to leave us wanting more fulfillment, so great is the enjoyment it provides. It lacks the physical impetus which pushes humans towards a search for the greater happiness of complete merging into Transcendence. It is from Transcendent stillness that angels emerge, just as the rest of humanity does, and only through knowing this will we know the Divine. In order to achieve it our intermediary should be Transcendence, ensuring there is no diversion. Any experience of angelic light should be understood as part of the world of physical form. Maharishi Mahesh Yogi[2], in Paul Mason's biography, says of this:

> The atmosphere about angels is so pretty that even though they have principally, and practically also, greater ability of performance and action, but their free will is hampered by the great prettiness of the atmosphere. Here in man the atmosphere is just enough to keep him hoping for more and more and more.

And Maharishi is also quoted as saying:

> Below man's species there are 8,400,000 species and then coming up to man… and then between man and God there is no record. Because we don't have to keep the record of all that we are going to bypass.

I have already spoken a little of the limitations of visualization techniques. Meditation on angels sounds fantastic. Done with an intense desire to go beyond them it would be helpful, but the truly sensational experience is the 'non-experience' of eternal, inner silence. It is from this that real healing takes place. What the woman's teaching meant to me was that in order to make a living, to be someone in the world, true spiritual wisdom had been shrunk. The fact is that we are only someone in the world when we know that we are no one. Then it is known that we are only Transcendence. In my opinion a great opportunity for wise teaching had been lost.

A week later I attended another day of workshops with the usual 'psychic equals spiritual' basis (discussed more in Chapter 7). There were many talks with no great spiritual depth to them. The last speaker was a young woman who talked about the huge amount of trite teachings in circulation which claimed to be spiritual. She spoke about her daily prayer and meditation and her belief in the possibility of a direct experience with what she called God. My heart lifted again; here was someone who seemed to have had a real spiritual encounter. She continued, however, to advocate a meditation which involved recalling and reliving the suffering of her every past life. This was in spite of the fact that prior to meditating she had not been consciously aware of it. During meditation she said she asked to relive and know past suffering; then she would tell herself she was finished with it and offer it to the Divine. The offering to the Divine of distress when it appears is a useful and appropriate response, but to request the re-emergence of hidden suffering seemed sad and unnecessary. There is enough distress to deal with anyway without desiring to know and re-experience more. She had said she did not believe that there was any need for an intermediary between human and Divine during meditation, yet by choosing to use a system of suffering she had established her past pain as her intermediary.

The investigation of past trauma without a Transcendent intermediary seems to be the essence of New-Age teaching. About 10 years ago a friend went to one of the most sought-after past- and present-life trauma therapists in the country. The first thing she was told was that she had cleared a huge amount of negativity herself. The reason was that she had practiced a Transcendent technique for years before arriving and it had liberated her from her past-life trauma and patterns. None of these had ever entered her present consciousness. This is the difference a consciousness-first technique makes. Furthermore, in an attempt to be understanding and all-embracing, New-Age thinking has placed much emphasis on the importance of the growth of the compassionate feminine. Not enough has been focused on discipline and effort. There is a marriage to be achieved between what is traditionally considered to be feminine tenderness and the more masculine discipline of rigorous systematic enquiry. In order to realize this Divine goal all the assistance that is available needs to be used: the essence of the compassionate blessing offered by the Avatar and the transmuting Grace of Transcendent teachings. They are one and the same. Determination is also vital. Spiritual development rests on awareness growing beyond all forms of phenomena past and present, from the dense physical world and its attendant suffering, to angels. And then to know the Source of them all. To achieve this more quickly there should be no intermediary but Transcendence.

There are no 'energies coming in' which are not already within, nothing which will take you further than your desires will allow.

7

Healing Pitfalls

New-Age magazines are full of articles and advertisements for sensational practices which promise unlikely results, often at the expense of the incorporation of Transcendence into awareness. In their desire for liberalism, and a compassionate empathetic attitude, members of the New-Age movement have incorporated into its teaching a large amount of 'spiritual' banality. The most common mistake is to elevate those practices, which lack the ability to expand awareness through transmutation, to an undeserved status. The result is nothing but an investigation of problems. I do not wish to analyze all of these but I have listed some of the most usual practices and accepted 'wisdom' generally encountered.

The Hypnotist

Some years ago I lived in Scarborough: a place full of talent and variety shows. While I was there a friend of mine went to see a hypnotist's show. The friend had gone on the second of two performances, as had the people chosen in the first show to be the hypnotist's subjects. Those who had participated in the previous night's performance were seated on the front row.

During the course of the performance, the people who had been chosen for their suitability were on stage, responding to the suggestions of the hypnotist and making fools of themselves for the benefit of the audience. Alarmingly, one of the women on the front row stood up and began to make 'clucking' noises and act like a chicken, reacting to the hypnotist's prompts in the same way as his subjects on the stage. She had continued to remain under the influence of his vibration, despite him having supposedly 'released' her from it, and was unconsciously complying with his wishes.

Obviously this is not the overt practice of New-Age therapists but it is a good example of how the vibration of one person's thought can be placed as a thought form into the energy field of another and, even more disturbingly, remain as an influence. Control is often discretely exercised. The influence of another's vibration, sometimes described as "exchange of energy", is subtly present in everyday life. It can be one subconscious method used in spiritual healing and may also affect mediums.

~ Other and Past-Life Aspects or Personalities ~ Attachments ~ Spirit Guides ~

Much is made within the spiritual healing world of other life aspects, personalities no longer incarnated into physical form: people who have, in our words, died, but are said to 'attach' themselves to the physical forms of those still living on the earth plane. Often called entities, attaching means that their close proximity affects the person they are drawn to. They may do this for many reasons but commonly to continue to experience the physical world and / or to gain influence within it. Often these life aspects are themselves unaware of their own clinging to those still living in the physical world. However, the biggest number of encounters with personalities from other lives that an individual, healer or otherwise makes are with their own. These exercise a hidden influence on behavior. They are an individual's own past-life aspects still existing and influencing the present: past personalities as real as the present one, yet usually unrecognized. Their influence may be spiritually evolutionary or not. Some will present themselves through the present personality as physical problems and the display of previous patterns of behavior. Others may have gained a degree of spiritual insight and so generate more positive, evolutionary inner impulses. During spiritual healing (where the energy of the healer is being used for healing) undesired life aspects may move from the recipient of the healing and attach themselves to the healer. But, despite their fears of attracting someone else's life aspects in this way, healers are often blind to the constant impulses of their own. Using the highest vibration of Transcendence during healing protects against inner and outer physical influences. It purifies both the healers' and the healees' less spiritually evolved life aspects.

I want to recount two experiences I had with other life aspects to shed some light on the inherent difficulties that can occur from dabbling in psychic activity when awareness is not clear. A few years ago a work colleague came to see me with her partner. Her partner had had persistent stomach problems and I offered to give him some healing. During the healing, with my inner vision, I saw the form of a small black being, minute in size, wearing a cape and a pointed hat. There was a connection of energy between this being and his stomach, in the form of a dark cord to his solar plexus, the stomach energy center (or third chakra). This life aspect had attached itself in order to gain some influence, and the physical effects of this resulted in his stomach discomfort. This small personality seemed to fly around me as I was healing, swirling in the most extraordinary circular movements and patterns. At the time I said nothing to either of them. My colleague had previously told me that she had a male guide who had been a monk who was always dressed in a brown cloak with a hood. After her partner's healing she recounted that she no longer had this monk as her guide. She also said she had received a reading from a psychic, during which a number of her new spirit guides had appeared in her vision, superimposed on top of the psychic's face. The psychic had been in a trance and told her he had 'channeled' these new guides through his own body. She went on to say that her partner also had a new guide and they believed it was 'Merlin' the magician. My colleague had asked her own new guides about this and had been informed that what she was seeing and understanding was correct, that her partner's new spirit guide was "Merlin indeed". I felt immediately unsettled by this news and was dubious about the validity of the reading she had received. I was sure this so-called magician was the life aspect I had seen during the healing and was positive it was the cause of the partner's stomach pain. I said nothing because I sensed that more information would emerge. I also felt there was some connection between the colleague's new guides and the emergence of 'Merlin'. I needed time to make more sense of the story. Later that evening the three of us meditated together. Inwardly during meditation I saw 'Merlin', now full-size and in the shape of an ordinary and elderly man. He was not emanating light; in fact his form was dark. He was casting what I understood to be negative, potentially harmful vibrations my way which I saw in the shape of black stars being thrown towards me. I also saw Mother Divine standing between myself and the black stars. When these thought forms sped towards me, she raised her hand and caught them. As she did this, the negativity within them was transformed and they changed into harmless stars of light. I felt completely unperturbed by this, knowing I was totally safe and could not be affected by any harmful intentions. The next day the three of us went for a walk together and my colleague continued to tell me how high the vibration of light her partner's magician guide was. Walking across a field together I began to think she was right and that I had been wrong. I saw out of the corner of my eye, behind her and her partner, the elderly man I had seen the day before. This time his form was not dark and dense but was emanating what appeared to be a pure vibration of light. He was projecting the appearance and light of an Avatar. But as I walked alongside he was unable to continue with this charade. In front of my eyes he turned again into what he really was: the very unpleasant old man I had seen previously. Driving home I was aware of him around the car, attempting to project his influence. Once more I knew that I was totally secure and that his lower vibration of light was unable to disturb my own.

After meditating that evening the colleague's original spiritual guide, the monk, came to me. He had much light. He asked me to tell the colleague that she had been connecting to a denser vibration of light by listening to the psychic's visitations and that the life aspect they had both thought was Merlin was not. The monk guide asked for my help. He was around her to help her with her spiritual evolution, but he was no longer able to because of her attraction to the information she had been given in the psychic's reading. The result of this was that she had not been able to see that the personality displaying itself as Merlin was false. This monk also told me that my own personal pathway would be lit. The next day I telephoned her and related what had happened in connection with 'Merlin' and the stories given to her through the trance work of the psychic. I asked her to do what her monk guide had requested and contact him after her meditation. She accepted this and later rang me to say she had done what had been asked. When she had contacted her true spiritual guide, the monk, he had told her that he radiated a higher vibration of light than the apparent guides which had influenced her via the psychic. After meditation that evening he again showed himself to me, to thank me. As he went to leave he bowed, swinging his cape around; when he did this he revealed that he was carrying a lamp. He turned and as he moved away he left behind him a pathway of light.

Another similar event occurred some months later with the same person. She told me one day that the monk guide was no longer with her again. During a guided visualization, facilitated by another psychic and intended to allow her to meet her spirit guides, my colleague had met yet another new guide. As she told me the story I saw the guide she was referring to. In my mind's eye this new guide appeared as a beautiful young Indian woman, one of the most enchanting I had ever seen, with emerald colored clothes and an emerald jewel carried in the middle of her forehead. She displayed herself as the Divine personality of an Avatar. As my thoughts rested on her stunning appearance, it changed dramatically. Beyond this facade was an old woman, not only unpleasant but potentially damaging. I said nothing as I did not feel it was the right time to question my colleague's judgment; I thought it would lead to anger. Traveling home I saw this personality had followed me and was trying to cause me harm. I was driving too fast for the road, was distracted by what I was seeing and suddenly felt a sharp jerk on the car wheel. I was fine, I did not lose control, but knew that was the moment when this life aspect had tried to exert her negative influence. She would have caused me harm had she been able to, the incline at the side of the road was very steep. On my return home I again saw the colleague's monk spirit guide who had contacted me previously. He confirmed my own ideas and suggested that I should say nothing of what I had seen to her; it would only increase her anger and this would cloud her vision further.

Many events took place that summer as I was daily healing this situation, including being aware of what I can only describe as spiritual meetings, where I felt like a child among spiritually wise elders. Towards autumn the monk came to me to say that he was again going to inwardly try to bring his light to my colleague. He wanted me to know that if he was unsuccessful he would remain by my side, continue to help me and so help her through me. The next day she rang me up in an unprovoked and angry state. She demanded furiously to know what I had seen of recent events; I felt I had no choice then but to tell the story. The Transcendent vibration I had used daily for months to help to heal this situation had exerted an effect. From that point onwards she began to see the cause of her anger and the unhelpful influences that had unconsciously been invited. A previous jealousy, hidden in one of her own latent past-life personalities, had been reignited. During this time she had met someone who had been a part of the same life who also held the same emotion. He too had quietly exerted an influence on her which had compounded the emotions of jealousy and anger. The negativity that began to express itself paved the way for further non-evolutionary influence to take hold of both of them in the form of fake spiritual guides. This resulted in the rejection of a positive, wise, safe and spiritually helpful one. Some years prior to this event this person had been warned by the Maharishi Jyotishees to take care over what she ingested. At the time we thought the advice was related to food intake. This was correct but it transpired it was also, and predominantly, to do with absorbing and being influenced by other people's negativity. The 'Merlin' personality of the first story had been a life aspect with an amount of spiritual learning but, still unenlightened, had opted for a crooked pathway which helped nobody spiritually. This story shows how one egotistical vibration attracts another. To have an unclear awareness is to perceive only a partial picture; it will perceive what it wants to see and emotions and motives of the self and others will be missed. Patanjali,[1] translated by Alistair Shearer, said of an unenlightened awareness:

> We should not respond with pleasure or pride to the alluring invitations of celestial beings, because this will obstruct progress, and it is always possible to fall.

Even people, who are considered to be spiritually developed in the eyes of others, may become fooled by beings they believe to be spirit guides. I have met people who live their lives solely on the say-so of their spirit guides. One woman springs to mind immediately. Her guides decided for her that she did not need to proceed with the spiritually evolving courses she had embarked upon. This was in spite of her own belief that what she had learnt had been beneficial. Such guides will lose their influence when spiritual awareness is at its height. Guides who many have handed over their power to, while appearing to help, may encourage stagnation. On spiritual healing courses if personalities appear, the instruction is for the spiritual healer to project their own inner light towards the life aspect they are encountering. This is taught to ensure it is a pure guide and there for the safety of the healer. But this teaching is no guarantee of clarity or protection. The vibrational quality of the light the spiritual healer is able to direct towards its object will determine how much protection and clarity is available to them.

Discernment grows with spiritual development. Perceiving influences and knowing whether they are spiritually helpful or not is the gain of Transcendent Awareness. At this stage the only enticement is Divine. No one is free of the influence of another person, nor will they see their hidden motives, until this state is achieved. In the presence of a pure vibration of light, denser light cannot hide. In higher states of consciousness the outer facade of behavior becomes transparent, and emotions and motives are seen. Clarity accompanies a vision which is founded on Transcendence; events then become lucid and subtleties of egotistical behavior obvious, their justifications visible. This does not mean that in enlightenment everything is known about everyone but it enables a helpful understanding in relation to pertinent life events and the greatest spiritual purpose behind events is manifest. Unconscious impulses which steer behavior, from past lives or other life aspects, stand out as a part of a continuum of patterns. Eventually the desire to use guides will be transcended. This refinement itself will ensure lucidity and that any communication which may take place with other life aspects is spiritually helpful.

~ Psychic Development ~

The single biggest flaw within the New-Age movement is the equating of psychic with spiritual. I have met many healers and mediums who consider themselves to be spiritual because they have a psychic capacity. Mediums and clairvoyants are people who have a particular ability in the same way as others have special skills, but 'being psychic' is not necessarily 'being spiritual'. Spirituality and psychic ability are not the same. Spirituality is the realization of Transcendent Awareness and maintaining it. While it is true that most people who develop spiritually will eventually gain a more penetrating, evolutionary and helpful awareness, a level of psychic knowing can be present which is not necessarily based on a full spiritual awareness. Psychics who claim to see pictures in their minds or hear voices may obtain only a limited amount of information. Based on this they give advice which may or may not be correct or helpful for the spiritual evolution of the person they are advising. Advice, however, which arises from an awareness which is complete has an inner, truly universal vision. Such information is based on actually *seeing* through a fully open third eye. Ramakrishna[2], in Christopher Isherwood's book, tells the story of a yogi showing off his psychic powers to a holy man. The holy man said to the yogi:

> "But what have you gained by having this power? Has it freed you from the wheel of death and rebirth? Will it save you from sickness and old age? Can it help you to realize God?" And, Christopher Isherwood continues: "The yogi was speechless. His understanding was awakened."

This should be the criterion; whatever the name given to Transcendence, the question which needs to be asked is: "Will what I am doing bring me to this liberation?" Even harboring the desire for a pure, simple, quiet life can become a distraction from spiritual activity, and so eventually an attachment. It does not therefore take much effort to imagine the sort of enticements the psychic arena holds. It is a big diversion, often compounded and justified by the mistaken belief that such activities are always spiritually enhancing. I have a friend who does not believe in any of the New-Age teachings; however, he said to me that there was one thing he knew about and that was plants. He claimed that he understood when a plant was unhappy and exactly why. The plants in his house are testimony to this. I have noticed he also has this faculty in relation to animals but he does not consider it to be outside the bounds of what he understands as normal. In the circles that I inhabit this ability would be named as psychic and such experiences as my friend's would be provided as evidence of possessing psychic gifts. His awareness is not a flashy experience, but is a part of his knowing; not from outside himself in the form of spirit guides, but from within. My friend does not display this ability to anyone; in over 30 years of knowing him he has mentioned it to me only twice. I believe him to have more awareness than many, with a perception which has expanded gradually to incorporate an *experience* of our underlying connection to plants and animals. It is quite feasible that someone without this connection, but with some psychic capacity, could have reached a similar understanding but only on an intellectual level. This is the difference between spiritual and psychic awareness.

Like attracts like is a truth. In daily life everyone attracts towards themselves what is a reflection of the vibration they generate. This is the creation of a physical reality, both individually and worldly. The kind of practice undertaken will reflect the consciousness of the individual who instigates it and it will have ramifications under this rule of attraction. As shown in the 'Merlin' story, if individual ego is predominant its vibration will attract a similar one and so be compounded. Ego attracts further ego, fear induces the creation of more potential for fear and a purer light will attract similar. Spiritual healers who, although believing themselves to be pure yet still have a strong individual ego, can attract unwanted vibrations, vibrations that they incorrectly believe they have the individual physical light to combat. In healing workshops I have heard reiki teachers say that they do not know how to help their students with their healing problems. Difficulties were often a result of a lack of protection in a healing process, where the reiki healer's individual vibration attracted and imbibed their clients' negativity. This does not always happen, but it is common, and when it does it is usually unconscious.

Obscurity in vision may also occur in relation to spiritual teachers, be they on the physical plane or another. The vibration of confidence and a determination to be seen as a guru generated by one who does not have the necessary spiritual learning is often absorbed by others who accept them as spiritual teachers. Individuals who are unable to see through the physical, emotional, material facade of the guru miss any hidden motives which may exist: motives which could be subconscious and not evolutionary. I have heard it said that there is no greater miracle than one in ignorance leading another towards enlightenment and herein lies the beauty of Transcendent techniques. As long as they are correctly taught it is possible for someone to learn to teach them precisely, irrespective of their own state of spiritual development. They make it possible for the blind to lead the blind. With such teachings even a teacher with ego or limited understanding is able to help another with their spiritual growth. Unless the teachers or spirit guides adhered to themselves have Transcendent Awareness, their understanding, and thus the information they give to those seeking it, will be restricted. This is true no matter how exceptional the information given seems. The leadership of guides who do have the expanded awareness of enlightenment has one purpose only: to steer the person they are guiding directly to their own experience of this greater awareness. Ramakrishna[3] (again in Christopher Isherwood's book) advised against becoming absorbed in mediumship practices, saying:

> ...if you let your mind dwell on ghosts, you'll become a ghost yourself. If you fix your mind on God your life will be filled with God. Now – which are you going to choose?

There is nothing wrong with seeking another's views and giving them consideration, on this physical plane or another. We do this daily. Spiritual development, however, is not based on an ability to communicate with those on other planes, but on whether or not the connecting stillness of Transcendence is maintained, even in the midst of daily action. Spiritual development is the process of becoming naturally Self-referential and assessing advice and information for ourselves. A referral to the small self of the individual grows, eventually to become a referral to the Transcendent Self. What we perceive from, Pure Awareness, comes through its incorporation into the perception of the individual form, to perceive itself everywhere, becoming Self-referring in the greatest sense. The negativity which lies within physical reactive light shrouds the pure light that it comes from. Dissolving it is the possibility of wise teaching. There is no method or teaching that will shed light on Transcendence. Transcendence is the light itself. Only because of this light are we able to experience the reactive light of physical creation. A Transcendent intermediary is a necessity.

In another mind-body-spirit exhibition I watched a young woman giving a talk about her courses in psychic development. She spoke with conviction; but unconsciously, contained and hidden, there was a great fear of what she was teaching. I was able to perceive inside her present physical form the shape of a fearful past-life aspect. The speaker had contained this personality into a small dark space within herself. She was attempting to overcome and prevent a previous fear from resurfacing. The problem? She was trying to do this by using the same method which had facilitated the creation of the fear in the first place. She was attempting to develop psychically without a sure foundation of spirituality. Rather than forcing psychic development she needed to melt her fear by going beyond it and practice real spiritual development, thus creating a naturally occurring psychic ability as a *result* of a growth in awareness. The quality of psychic perception depends upon the spirituality, and so discrimination, of the knower. Again, wisdom depends on awareness. When awareness is attached to physical forms such as the mind, emotions, past and future, it is restricted. A spiritual awareness which has become pure and clear incorporates non-experience, what is beyond all experience, beyond words and without boundaries. The value of this non-experience was illustrated to me during a conversation with someone who had spent time with Maharishi Mahesh Yogi in Switzerland attending an extended meditation course. He told me about his experience one afternoon after meditating when the course participants were asked to discuss their meditations with Maharishi. One by one they stood up and listed experience after wonderful experience. Sensational stories of, among other things, visions of angels were related. This man told me that he had felt that he had no such experience to share and that he had told Maharishi this. Despite this Maharishi insisted that he stand up and relate what had happened to him during his meditation. He complied and said that he had nothing special to tell, except that at the start of his meditation he had been irritated by a truck which had been driving up and down the street by the side of his window. Eventually, he told his audience, the sound of the truck ceased to irritate him and disturb the peace of his meditation. At the end of the hour he had reached the point where he had begun to enjoy its sound. Maharishi responded by telling everyone present that this tale was the only Divine experience he had heard that day: a story of something which gave pain but turned around to bring bliss.

One of the most aware people I know claims to have never had a psychic encounter. As with my other friend, who understands plants and animals, she says that she is not able to see or hear anything psychically. But every response and observation she makes I believe is from a level of substantial spiritual steadiness. Although she is not yet experiencing the higher states of awareness (discussed later in Chapter 11) she has gradually expanded her perception from many years of using a Transcendent technique. It is vital to understand that if additional abilities develop, even as a result of spiritual progress, these may only be temporary. Becoming entangled and attached to these capacities and failing to cherish the goal of enlightenment may actually impede progress. Sri Aurobindo[4] said that there is no wisdom which is ultimately not within but Robert A. McDermott quotes him when he also warned about the possibilities of awareness not being clear:

> Cease inwardly from thought and word, be motionless within you… Then will Truth dawn on you from above and flow in you from all around you.
>
> But only if the mind is no less intense in its purity than its silence. For in an impure mind the silence will soon fill with misleading lights and false voices, the echo or sublimation of its own vain conceits and opinions or the response to its secret pride, vanity, ambition, lust, greed or desire. The Titans and the Demons will speak to it more readily than the Divine Voices.

~ Sensitivity ~

The speaker on psychic development mentioned above also spoke about certain sensitivity problems often experienced by what she called 'sensitives' or psychics. She began to explain spiritual evolution in terms of an inability to cope. For me this is not an acceptable expectation. It is a received notion that I have encountered often within spiritual healing organizations; that spiritual development inevitably involves some hypersensitivity which will result in it becoming a nuisance to life and in a loss of usual physical capacity. Very often they suggest this takes the form of food intolerance. I would go so far as to say, unpopular though it may be, that it is almost a badge of honor. To have a food intolerance is commonly seen as a sign of being a 'sensitive' and is equated with spiritual development. In other words: a sign of evolution is the loss of ability to enjoy certain food. This psychic speaker continued to list the endless number of complaints that might be experienced as a result of the psychic development she referred to as spiritual. The seemingly inevitable outcome of this is that someone will become a physical wreck, unable to enjoy their lives, by the time they are fully evolved. Her teaching of practices such as visualizing opening energy centers, without a spiritual practice which ensures they open in a spontaneous and evolutionary manner, allows a greater chance of undesirable vibrations entering rather than a pure one. Visualizing opening energy centers, of the healer and the person being healed, is common among spiritual healers. But deliberately opening undeveloped centers leaves them vulnerable. Again, protection is as sound as the spiritual evolution of the healer dictates. Any increase in sensitivity needs to be matched by a practice which increases resilience and safety. The chakras must be developed in an evolutionary fashion (how this is done is described in Chapter 9). In the highest spiritual state the five senses become so strong they activate the experience of bliss. With this capacity, no matter what food is eaten (even though it may not be the most desirable food), bliss is created in the eater. An unpleasant smell, while still not pleasant or desired by the mind, will create bliss within. Hearing, sight, sound, taste and smell, in enlightenment, awaken the Transcendent vibration of their object. Perfect human consciousness creates joy and a perception of the Divine within the senses. This happens no matter what that object is. Clearly there are food preferences for everyone; the wisdom preserved in a pure Ayurvedic system informs us of this. I question, however, the emphasis on intolerance and its inevitability as a feature of evolution. Buddha was purported to have said that the words that emerge from the mouth are of more consequence than what is ingested through it. It is more important for speech and the vibration behind it to be pure, than food. Eating what is offered by a host, even when not enjoyed, does less harm spiritually than refusing the food and so offending them. It seems to me that the current focus on sensitivity and food is a part of the all-pervasive attachment to body image that is so prevalent. Its correlation with spiritual development is a misunderstanding. There is nothing in the journey to enlightenment which means progressive loss; this idea comes from an understanding not grounded in Transcendence. There is not even a loss of individual ego; rather, an individual's ego grows to become a reflection of Divine impulses. Such growth means that an individual's actions are naturally generated from unconditional love, compassion and desire for spirituality.

~ Past Lives ~

I have already touched upon past lives and the difference a consciousness-first approach makes to releasing the emotional and mental patterns held as a result of experiences. What we place our attention on grows and, as we are already holding painful past patterns, it seems to me wholly undesirable that the woman mentioned earlier who meditated on them created an intermediary which facilitated the experience of more discomfort. In this dense and unenlightened world there is an enormous demand for sensationalism and an almost non-existent one for enlightenment. Never is this more clearly demonstrated than in the huge amount of New-Age interest in past lives. This fascination has become a distraction. We never have to revive the past in order to heal it. Even if it investigates the root of the problem from a previous life, spiritual assistance must involve an intermediary which liberates. It will not help the sufferer to treat the past as the cause of their unhappiness, nor to run the risk of becoming attached to it. We cannot hope to clear our systems of every past trauma by the reliving of it, it is a physical impossibility. Attempting this is both unpleasant and impossibly fraught with pitfalls. Investigating what emanates from consciousness in order to change is too painful and too lengthy; it diverts and clouds the mind. What are past lives if not the creation of past form to which an individual has become attached? The investigation of past-life aspects is nothing more than the investigation of past illusion.

When an individual misses an opportunity for liberation and reincarnates, there is no guarantee about the quality of their future life. If they are comfortable now, they may not be in such a delightful position again for hundreds, even thousands of lives. Who knows what karma is waiting in the wings? It is also possible that the challenges they have created for themselves may not appear for a similar amount of time. If, in the next lifetime, an individual who has an interest in investigating past incarnations continues to do so, what might they be analyzing? The answer could be: the life they are living now. When doing so they may realize that in this life they could have taken the leap to develop spiritually. Alternatively they may be blaming their past lives for their present situation. An intellectual insight is not the full realization necessary to go beyond present or past form. It is not an understanding on the level of the mind which will release painful patterns, far from it; attachments made by the mind are the source of problems. Trying to solve them by using the instrument of the mind, the instrument which created them, is futile. The reason anyone seeks help is because they are experiencing difficulties in the present. An individual, now, holds all their past-life personalities within this existence. Only in a higher state of awareness will they perceive them as the continuum they really are. With Pure Awareness in perception past lives are cognized simultaneously and past personalities are lived alongside the current one. One with an interest in the intellectual understanding of what they have created earlier may look at it, but cling to past form, and an attachment to it will be the result. *Saturating the mind and emotions with past pain cannot be healing and it may render a person unable to fully appreciate the present.*

Liberation brought about through an expansion of awareness releases; then it is possible that an intellectual understanding may instantaneously arise in the mind. In order to be released from held past impressions and patterns of behavior, whenever they were created, it is imperative to seek out those therapists who use Transcendent healing techniques. Even more beneficial would be the learning of these techniques by clients themselves. Many practices are described as having the capacity to transmute when they do not. Furthermore, taking time to work back through the pain which has been created is time during which different problems and further suffering may arise.

Achieving Transcendent Awareness brings with it wisdom of the dream-like quality of the reactive light in which all lives are lived. From this enlightened viewpoint identification with any life aspect, past or present, is appreciated as nothing but delusion. Without Transcendence delusion investigates itself. If an individual is unable to disengage from their present life, what makes them think they will behave differently when it comes to past lives? Why add more illusion and suffering to cling to? Investigating past lives while using the precision of Transcendence ensures a healing which heads in the direction of karmic release. Without this there is no guarantee that, even though physical change takes place, perception will increase in subtlety and strength.

~ Suffering ~

I am not suggesting that we will never suffer; there will be times of the spontaneous emergence of painful emotions. But, no matter how grateful for the outcome of any painful experience, few of us would wish to revisit and re-experience the pain of it. Given a choice, most of us would have preferred an easier route to the present circumstances in which we live. Routes of spiritual development which invite suffering exist because individuals are attached to their pain. *But a belief in suffering dismisses the transmutation that Transcendent Grace offers.* Buddha said that all life lived through a limited awareness is suffering. A good and comfortable life is only a good life in comparison to other less content or happy lives. Each life lived not knowing Transcendence is a life of poverty in comparison to living it with this consciousness. We have all heard of those who despite being wealthy ended their own lives, suffering in spite of their comfortable material condition. How absurd this must seem to some of those in developing countries who live lives of abject poverty; that the comparatively easy living conditions in the West do not ensure complete happiness. Real wealth is the gold of spirituality. This will provide an inner foundation of fulfillment from which to enjoy physical circumstances and it is the only value we take with us when we die. Everyone has their own preferred pathway, but if a teaching states that suffering is necessary, it is advisable to look at this teaching again. The simple act of experiencing Transcendence and its Grace is the pathway of joy.

~ The Movement of Vibration ~

The practice of channeling light and removing a client's unwanted vibrations, by visualizing placing it into the earth, is the teaching of many spiritual healing organizations. In the present green climate we berate ourselves about the chemical pollution we put into the ground, yet spiritual healers give no thought to the negativity they deposit into the earth. The world is overloaded with this psychic pollution, and, contrary to the received wisdom, I do not believe the earth alone transmutes it.

It is possible to generate healing from endlessly varying levels of vibration and consciousness. Alongside the relevance of the point (made in Chapter 5) that awareness is filtered through an individual and their spiritual discernment depends on this, was the point that any action can be generated by either a spiritually supportive or non-evolutionary vibration. No matter how effective it looks on the surface, a healing may not be generated from a pure vibration of intent. The quality of vibration used in any seemingly miraculous healing will determine how supportive of evolution that healing is (this is discussed in greater depth in Chapter 9). The vibration which instigates healing will vary from the wide range of individual ego to genuine compassion. Without the use of a truly pure vibration, one that emerges from outer physical reactive light may nevertheless promote the removal of a client's difficulties. But what happens to these unhelpful vibrations will also vary and the possibilities are endless. On the spiritual healing courses I have attended, prior to beginning their healing, trainees were taught to connect to the earth through visualization by putting roots from their feet down into the soil (as in the earlier story of the woman conducting the angelic meditation). This practice leaves healers, as well as meditators who use a similar visualization, open to attracting denser vibrations already held within the earth. They are taught at the same time to open their energy centers and therefore run an increased risk of this happening. Although I had no need to use spiritual healing techniques, I once tried this. Immediately I saw and felt a large gold block being placed under the soles of my feet and gold vibrations radiating up my legs. I knew not to continue. It was clear to me that such a practice was not helpful and my healing was best served by the activation of a Transcendent vibration. I have watched spiritual healers using this method and seen a client's vibrations being 'chased' by physical light and disappear into the earth. Healers who remove such vibrations from their clients by using their own physical system are leaving themselves vulnerable. Not only are they making themselves susceptible to the effects of the energy they absorb into their bodies, but they are adding to the energetic pollution of the planet. It is the function of the earth to hold and reflect humanity's earthly karma and, if deemed right by reactive light law, to return it. This law applies for both individuals or groups. Natural disasters are the result of a purification of the planet on a large scale. But they create suffering and the possibility of holding onto impressions from more emotional pain. Just as it is not desirable to add more chemicals to a polluted ocean, so it is with psychic impurity.

Other spiritual healers have told me that they are moving energy around the body of the person being healed in an attempt to balance energy centers (or chakras). A healer once tried to do this to me, telling me I had been "doing too much meditating". He was unable to see what the distribution of my vibrations reflected. He tried to move the energy located in the top energy center (the crown chakra) and move it into a lower one. This was not a success but inherent within this activity is the possibility of spreading lower vibrational energy. Doing this may move the seeds of any existing problems (such as emotional, mental problems or even physical disease) into a different energy center. The potential for possible future problems may be latent and not yet visible. Problems spread may rise into an individual's awareness at a much later date, even in a future life. I have met clients who have been made aware of feelings of fear and anxiety through this method of healing.

Awakening Fear

At a recent mind-body-spirit event I watched some spiritual healers at work. In order to give the person being healed a direct experience of higher consciousness they were attempting to raise kundalini energy. Kundalini energy is a spiritual life-energy located at the bottom of the spine. During the process of spiritual development it is said to unfold and rise steadily in the body, purifying and making each energy center more aware. When the kundalini reaches the top chakra, and is retained, a person is said to be enlightened. It seemed to me that, in an attempt to force the rising of the kundalini and heal their client's denser physical vibrations, they had only disturbed them. Unwanted vibrations which were lodged in a lower position were either being placed into a more aware higher one, or at least being uprooted and awakened. The healers also appeared to be 'tying knots' around the throat area in the energy system of the person being healed. It was quite an exciting-looking practice which was drawing plenty of attention. I was at the exhibition with a friend who is able to see energy and I asked her to watch it. When she did it made her feel physically sick.

Not long after this I met someone who had also attended this event. She told me that she and her friend had received healing at this stand. While she had "not felt right" since her healing, her companion had suffered some very obvious side-effects. The friend had endured constant nightmares and a steady feeling of unease during the day. The healers had disturbed a fear and in doing so had brought it into conscious awareness. It was a fear the client might never have needed to know about. Had a technique that touched her with Transcendence been used instead, her fear might have been transmuted before ever entering her present awareness. An evolutionary meditation prepares the chakras to gradually maintain a higher vibration and in doing so melts hidden problems. I have no doubt the healers were well-intentioned and what they were doing was exercised in the name of spiritual development. But, like a disease, a fear had been spread, and the resultant distress had been unnecessary.

In some spiritual healings, healers do not visualize putting the lower vibrations they attract into the earth but leave them around the healing space; where they remain either to return to the client or, in some cases, latch onto somebody else. When I watch healers who do not use a Transcendent intermediary, I often see the denser vibrations they have attracted left behind. (In the company of an Avatar this action would be acceptable. Their Transcendence would purify by generating its vibration into the environment, raising the vibrations of those around them.) Many times I have used my Transcendent techniques to raise the lower vibrations that I have seen left inside a healing room by spiritual healers, apparently unaware of what they have done.

Some spiritual healers believe that rather than channeling or depositing others' unwanted vibrations, they have the physical capacity to absorb and purify them. These particular healers believe they themselves can transmute using their own energy. Once again they are leaving themselves susceptible to the energy of their client and to any life aspects which may be present. A healer adopting the negativity which is not theirs may allow the person being healed some breathing space from their problems. But, as with the denser matter transferred into the earth, unless these lower vibrations are transmuted they will eventually return to the physical system of the person who generated them. It is a fundamental law, embodied in the arena of reactive light, that individuals have responsibility for their actions and actions have effects and ramifications. It is the law of karma and only Grace in the form of the Avatar or a Transcendent vibration has the power to release individuals from it. Consciously or subconsciously absorbing another's negativity is an unwise practice. I have known spiritual healers who were constantly unwell from this practice.

Only Avatars have the body to withstand this sustained procedure, yet even they have to find their physical limitations; they cannot heal everyone of everything. The Avatar Ramakrishna[2] blamed the throat cancer that killed him on the impurities he had absorbed from his devotees. His absorption of these devotees' impurities resulted in them being released from their unwanted karma. His pure physical system had the capacity to transmute it and ensure it did not return to its instigator. Avatars are Transcendence, beyond the realms of normal human suffering, and even after their death their vibration continues to purify. Hence the spiritual significance of the sites in which they lived their lives. They become places of worship and healing. Nevertheless it is still a necessity that those who go to them give consent, and surrender to this Divine Grace. Sometimes Avatars allow themselves to suffer physically, but this suffering is different to the pain experienced by the unelightened. Jesus did this on the cross and in doing so relieved humanity of much painful karma. The result of the absorption of dense, impure vibrations was throat cancer for Ramakrishna. The causes and purposes of illness in the Avatar are very different to those which lie behind the suffering of others. But, if cancer was the result for Ramakrishna, how can less spiritually developed healers expect to not be affected when using only their own physical form for healing?

Women are particularly vulnerable to the absorption of another's vibrations. With their nervous systems, they often relieve those close to them of pain, albeit temporarily. It is because of this faculty that they are deemed to make good nurses and carers; they help sick people who are near them feel better and their maternal role may render them more sensitive to a child's or patient's needs. It is this faculty (used as evidence of an ability to rally unseen forces) that was used by some in previous ages to label certain women witches. The love of the woman as carer, her empathy and her wish to remove suffering, coupled with the greater vulnerability of her more sensitive nervous system, leaves her particularly open to the absorption of another's vibration. It is because of her sensibility to this movement of energy that women are more likely to become spiritual healers. Today spiritual healing organizations are predominantly constituted of females, this in spite of the fact that the spiritual healers who are deemed to be successful and given the most publicity are men. However, a woman being a good nurse from the patient's point of view may not necessarily be helpful for her own physical well-being. Any shedding of dense vibrations by the person being healed could be described as healing. It is not helpful to hold onto problems and releasing them, even temporarily, allows space for a spiritual understanding to develop. The experience of even an impermanent healing facilitates an increase in awareness, a consciousness of something in existence which is unseen, and an easier life can make it more conducive to pursuing this spiritual growth. But, if the dense vibrations behind the source of the problem are not transmuted, they will return to the awareness of their instigator, possibly in another form, and if not in this lifetime, in another. This is often a slow, painful and confusing process for the person who created the karma. The law of karma is simple: the effects of whatever vibrations created by individuals (through thoughts, words and deeds) must return to them unless dissolved by exposure to the blessing of Transcendence. Only a Transcendent intermediary will effect true change. Women need the support of Transcendent healing techniques for the benefit of themselves and others. I hope also that the time has come for men to accept their own capacity to work with Transcendence; when this happens healing will become more accepted socially. Both men and women using a subtle vibration for the purpose of spiritual upliftment for everyone will bring a greater understanding of male and female vibrations. These are equal in status and permeate both sexes.

~ Mediumship ~ Trance Work ~

One common practice, among mediums in particular, is that of channeling other life aspects, sometimes while in a trance. This involves the medium consciously allowing (although it can happen spontaneously and subconsciously also) a different life aspect to take control of their body in order for them to speak their guidance. Of necessity this means that the consciousness of the medium is withdrawn from the senses, giving the incoming personality control of the medium's physical functioning. Sometimes this is done completely, resulting in the medium's consciousness leaving their physical body totally. During this activity it is not unusual for the medium to speak in a different language or adopt the accent or appearance of the being they are channeling. Psychic surgeons are well-known for channeling entities. It is a process which must inevitably create strain on the body of the individual who encourages it to happen to them. It provides a justification for abdicating responsibility, as the medium is allowing someone else to speak through them, they themselves do not have to accept responsibility for what they are saying. The single most unhelpful, and potentially damaging, New-Age practice is that of allowing another personality to invade personal physical space. It is neither helpful nor advisable for anyone to permit another being to take control over them, or use their body in any way, and it is a practice which is best avoided. I have heard that this ability to channel other life aspects is seen as a sign of becoming spiritually developed in spiritual healing and mediumship circles, but nothing could be further from the truth. The reasons for this sort of trance or channeling practice vary but from any intention it makes the absorption of lower vibrations possible and may be physically harmful. As with healers who absorb the vibrations of others and are totally unable to transmute them, I have seen mediums become seriously ill, once even suicidal, from this practice.

Communicating with a high vibration through unbounded Transcendence is a wholly different experience.

~ Astral Traveling ~

For the same reason as trance work, creating a situation which may result in being overcome by other life aspects (such as the practice of astral traveling) is also best avoided. Astral traveling is the process of consciousness and mind and subtle body (often called the astral body) being removed from the physical body completely. Existing in a state of suspension and separation, yet remaining in connection with their physical form. Astral travelers describe themselves as literally "flying" above events and places. They watch their own body, while they hover above it, attached by what is often described as a "life-cord". Unlike knowing outer phenomena from an integrated awareness infused with Transcendence, the activity of astral traveling is *dis*integrating. It is a total separation of an individual's consciousness and their physical reactive light body. This is the opposite of spiritual expansion. It is also a means by which physical karmic events are avoided. Two stories relating to this spring to mind. The first is about a friend who began to astral travel so regularly she was unable to stop doing it. It started to terrify her as it began to happen without her conscious intent and without warning. Eventually she sought help and was told that she had created a tear in her aura by, at first, deliberately taking her awareness through it. The second story is about a spiritual healer who left her body.

Tanya's Traveling

A friend had organized a spiritual healers' workshop in her home and, ever interested, I joined in. It was designed to help people see each other's auras. One by one we had to sit on a chair at the front of the group.

Tanya took her turn to be the center of attention. As soon as she sat down her face was covered in small dark shadows which were flickering around her. It looked deeply unpleasant. Later in the evening she talked about how she could "travel" to places and attract other life aspects which were "stuck" in their density. She believed that she could show them her light, which would draw them towards her, and then encourage them to head towards a purer light and so healing. This is not an unusual practice in spiritual healing circles and spiritualist churches. Clearly these personalities had gone nowhere but had remained around her, no doubt affecting in some way her own well-being. She also complained about how her own physical energy affected the working of electrical machinery in her home.

I came to know Tanya better and she later related an astral traveling experience. She told me that she had once been very ill and quite without conscious intent (although I am sure with an unconscious one) she left her body. Away from the physical arena she encountered two other life aspects which she thought were her spirit guides. They told her that they wanted to take her to purer light to teach her and they convinced her that she should go with them. She was just about to do this when suddenly she realized that they were not there to guide her at all. She began to panic and tried to get back into her body, but had great difficulty doing so. These entities did everything they could to stop her and a struggle ensued in which Tanya fortunately managed to overcome them. She was able to return her consciousness and subtle body to her gross physical body.

Tanya did not appear to have learned anything from her experience. It had been obvious at the aura workshop that she had continued to attract undesirable life aspects; furthermore, she was neither healing them nor was she impervious to their effect. The influence and advice of guides is not usually intended to be harmful, but when a lesser vibration interferes (as seen in the earlier stories of the life aspects) subtle misinformation is the result. This will affect spiritual development.

The life aspects in Tanya's story had wanted to control her body for their own purposes. Like pirates overtaking a boat, other discarnate personalities can overshadow, or completely overcome, the consciousness of another to utilize their body for themselves. It is possible the karmic quality of the life-thread (referred to in Chapter 3) can be severed; this allows the subtle body to wander in a different plane, free of the ramifications from previous action. Hence some people suddenly show signs of a dual personality or display dramatic atypical, often violent, behavior (although this is by no means the usual reason for such behavior). Astral traveling is not a spiritually evolutionary habit. We have created dense physical existence from outer reactive light and in order to allow its expression, and experience the result of this, we must be in a corresponding physical, outer reactive light body. It is an attachment to the desires existing within an individual which prompts the initial act of incarnation; withdrawing awareness from the physical body results in a suspension from the pending karmic events which emanate from these. What real spiritual growth is gained by this? It is an experience which lies within the field of the sensational and not the genuinely spiritual. The activity of floating above the body is not integrating a greater awareness, quite the opposite. On spiritual healing courses I have met healers who practice astral traveling during the act of spiritual healing, leaving both themselves and their recipient vulnerable. When, instead, the whole universe is experienced within, the world and its outer phenomena are known in an evolutionary way. Avoiding the sensationalism of non-evolutionary customs, and aiming for the experience of blissful Divine union, is genuinely sensational.

~ Visualization and Channeling Light Healings ~

Alice Thomson in her interview with the Dalai Lama[5] said:

> He laughs when I change the subject and talk about the West's attempts to become more spiritual through yoga, massage and acupuncture. "These are just physical activities," he says. "To be happier, you must spend less time plotting your life and be more accepting."

The New-Age movement has given voice to an important development in understanding: that we create from within, through thought, our outer reality. Therefore, in the absence of effective awareness-enhancing techniques, the New-Age solution to creating a better life is to change thought. An enormous amount of time is spent on this and visualization techniques form its basis. The belief is that producing different thoughts will produce a different life and a different consciousness. It is, however, impossible to change the underlying vibration and spiritual quality of thoughts unless creating simultaneously an inner experience of the connecting point of stillness from where they come. Only from this Source level can the quality of thoughts be efficiently restructured. Most visualization practices which are deemed to work are due more to an emerging change of awareness rather than vice versa and it is this which may prompt the desire for outer help. But this change may have taken aeons to emerge. Reshaping physical form has more effect when done from the most powerfully pure level in existence, that of Transcendence. Again I am suggesting here that New-Age understanding is mistaking what is the *effect* of spiritual expansion as a route to it. Reshaping behavior is encouraged as a means to gaining a better life, unlike a consciousness-first approach which spontaneously brings about changes. It is important to watch conduct and to make attempts to improve, but in the absence of awareness-altering techniques the effort needed to do this will outweigh permanent achievements. This has been highlighted already in the example of the yo-yo dieter, constantly alternating between positive and negative action, and struggling with both. Positive, evolutionary thought and behavior is a *result* of being established in a state where the mind has gained infinity, where individual awareness has become pure and reflects Transcendence. One example of this is the desire to move house and seek freedom from noisy neighbors. Moving house without transmuting the karma that is the cause of the problem may only result in temporary escape. The issue could well resurface at a later date, and its nuisance element could emerge in a different shape and package. It may be a different event, involving different people. If, however, a house move is made as a consequence of the transmutation of the patterns which created the emergence of the nuisance, then the move will be successful. In fact, once such karmic conditions have been negated, there may be no need to move at all. Important as it is to be happy in a physical surrounding, creating a better physical life, and clinging to it, will cause spiritual stagnation. Watching behavior is beneficial, as is attempting compassion and service, but like a house built on sand, creating a better life without the solid inner foundation of spiritual wisdom and fulfillment will be a life of instability. Behavior generated from living individuality but with Transcendent Awareness creates spontaneously both a harmless and joyful existence.

In the healing and meditation circles that I have inhabited, meditation generally means one thing only: visualization. As I have shown previously there is no such thing as healing only endlessly different forms of healings. This sentiment is also applicable to meditations. The difference between techniques which access a vibration directly from Transcendence and practices such as visualization which utilize physical reactive light is enormous. Visualizations are another creation of the mind. As emotions and thoughts are considered to be the basis for the sort of life an individual has, so visualization, through thought, attempts to realize a different life experience. Visualizing means utilizing the world of imagination and its vibrational quality will, yet again, depend on the state of spiritual awareness of its creator. The range will be from a denser experience to that of Transcendent light in one who is awake. The experience of visualization may be enjoyable but, without the addition of a pure vibration to draw attention towards Transcendence in order to go beyond the physical, its facility to expand consciousness is limited. The process of visualizing is an act which lies in the realms of the mental. A more effective practice goes beyond the mind, and reaches a stillness which is out of the reach of thought. Invoking images is an activity which rests in the aspect of life which includes physical phenomena.

It was probably in the late 1970s / early 1980s, when I had been meditating for a number of years, I was sent on a job-related workshop. The facilitator created a time for relaxation. This was the first time I had come across visualization techniques and I was baffled by the reaction of others on the course. I found it hard to understand how they had thought that the visualization experience was real relaxation. While there was a certain alleviation of physical sensations, I did not find that the mental activity involved encouraged complete stillness. A friend later pointed out that I was probably the only person on the course who knew the experience of Transcendence. As usual, its potential for widening the still space between thoughts had been my benchmark. It is possible when using visualizations to reach a pleasant, more attractive 'place', but still the mind is utilized. Nowadays visualization techniques are thought to develop those using them spiritually; in fact they are often enhancing a faculty which could more accurately be described as psychic. Only if it takes the aspirant beyond the clutches of the mind can an activity be described as spiritual. Going a little way towards it is not enough and may cause blocks to development as attachments to this type of meditation can easily be formed. Visualizations encourage phenomena and are another attempt to change behavior without necessarily changing consciousness. New-Age workshops are full of people describing and analyzing their inner visions and messages and in this situation the discernment of the workshop facilitator becomes paramount. It is completely possible to be entranced by these experiences and become stuck in a half-way house of the mind. There is much scientific evidence to support this view. Research on deeper meditative states beyond the activity of the mind has shown the brain to function differently. There is greater harmony between the left and right sides of the brain, a harmony which is not visible in other states such as visualization. Visualization techniques are no more a sure experience of Transcendence than physical therapies like aromatherapy or reflexology. These therapies help to bring some soothing of the body that may aid a deeper meditation, but it is essential to go further. Creating beautiful visions during meditation is fascinating, that moment will be enjoyed; but like the world it is transient and will not fulfill totally. Going beyond visualization meditations, even those in which light is visualized and channeled, is a must for individual awareness to expand. The vibration of any light that is channeled will only be made up of the vibrations an individual is spiritually developed enough to produce. Visualizing, and becoming attached to an illusory light-world, is a conceivable outcome of a meditation which depends on channeling light. Desiring to know the Source of light is more helpful. It is even feasible that being submerged in long states of bliss during meditation can become an attachment and so a subtle obstacle. The Source and essence of bliss has to be known.

It is not images and visions when meditating which determine a level of spiritual development, but the expansiveness of awareness. When this becomes a reference point from which reactions and decision-making is made. This is especially so at times of stress and crisis. The only really helpful spiritual visualization is to visualize, in whatever way is possible, God. But only in order to go beyond the form of the visualization.

~ Signs ~

Looking for signs of our own spiritual development is like constantly opening the oven door to see if a cake is rising. Given this treatment it will never rise. Looking for, and grasping at, signs of individual development is a common stumbling block to spiritual growth. Awareness grows, and like breathing it is mostly steady and unnoticed. Searching for signs, either of how to behave or for confirmation of previous behavior, is an activity packed with potential pitfalls.

I once met a young woman who had been diagnosed with throat cancer and was refusing orthodox treatment. Her consultant wanted her to undergo further tests prior to her considering having her tumor removed. She was understandably terrified. On the two days she had an appointment for the tests she felt too ill to travel to the hospital. While trying not to influence her final decision, I encouraged her to have these investigations before she made a definite choice about whether or not to undergo surgery. I suggested that the test results would give her more information on which to base her decision. She refused, saying that the fact that she had been ill on both of the days they were due was a definite "sign" that she was not to have them done and that she should not consider an operation. From my perspective I saw these signs differently. I thought that she was subconsciously creating the temporary illness in order to give herself a reason for not having the tests and possible subsequent surgery. Her 'sign' was a reflection of her fear and reluctance. It was this all-pervasive fear in her which had expressed itself as her temporary illness, and so her sign. Not only had it clouded her rational thinking process, it had provided her with a justification for her decision. She had brought an alternative reality into being. The decision she made may have been the right one for her, it is not for me to judge, but, on the surface level of her mind she had created a situation which rationalized her unconscious impulses and expressed her understandable dread. This woman never went for tests or surgery, she died of her cancer and died in great fear.

Signs are dependent on interpretation. The accuracy of the interpretation will depend on the clarity and extensiveness of perception. Understanding any situation, whether it is seen as a sign or not, will depend on the wisdom of an individual's vision. Again, spiritual discernment correlates to awareness. Considering something in life to be a sign is 'reading' an individual's creation, their identity and reality. An interpretation may be spiritually supportive or it may not; either way perceiving what has been created as a sign compounds this reality. Individuals unconsciously recreate scenarios, and place themselves into situations, which compound their world-view. Analyzing these scenarios and situations, past or present, adds yet another layer to their personal story: a story which is in fact illusory.

~ Presence and Now ~ Mindfulness ~ Pathless Teachings ~

The terms 'being present', 'living for now' or 'in the moment', and 'behaving mindfully' have become common teaching among those who make up the New-Age movement. It is here, where the gulf between the state of consciousness of the Self-realized teacher and the understanding their followers have of the teaching, shows most of all. Followers of those in an enlightened state of consciousness can only understand the descriptions of these states from their own level of wakefulness. Their receptivity is determined by their awareness. In the hands of those who have no experience of higher states of consciousness (described later in Chapter 11) statements such as 'being in the now' are overused and misunderstood phrases which, when utilized, embody little relevance to their potential spirituality. They have become empty refrains which appear regularly and have now permeated mainstream culture. This is a further example of what is the *outcome* of enlightenment being mistaken as a *method* of achieving it. 'Mindful behavior', 'being present' and 'living in the moment' are understood as methods of achieving enlightenment. Knowing presence, now, and mindfulness, however, is a *result* of living it. Living in these states of consciousness is the maintenance of Transcendent Awareness; an inner observing of physical activity from Pure Awareness, this is knowing presence, the now and mindfulness. A state of mindfulness might better be called mindlessness but this would also be misunderstood and does not mean that the mind is not used or useful (this experience is described in Chapter 11). In enlightenment individual awareness becomes pure, direct and lucid, free from the clutter of the mind. Many meditation teachers teach a mindful meditation, with the intention of creating greater mindfulness in the meditator of objects such as the chair they are sitting on. And in other methods the teaching is to become more aware of the events taking place around the student. This is not the real meaning or experience of mindfulness but a restricted understanding of what is a high state of awareness. These are watered down, limited teachings which have often been misunderstood by the teacher. Take any expression used to describe presence, now and mindfulness and know that it is not that. Teachers who live in a higher state of consciousness will always try to explain it, but they can never be fully understood other than on the level of experience. Describing living presence, now and mindfulness, with no specific means of achieving it, may even deepen misinterpretation. When awareness begins to incorporate more of the Transcendent vibration of presence, greater clarity is a possibility. But an individual's awareness will not be mindful until it fully maintains Transcendence. The difficulty is that, without a specific technique, presence is really difficult to achieve. Often people tell me that they are unable to meditate, that they try to experience presence and live in the now, but find it too tough. They are searching for something, yet often do not know what or where that something is. In spite of the descriptions of states of greater fulfillment, having no prior taste of it, or means by which they can be introduced to it, they struggle. Many flounder completely and give up. Without the direct infusion of expansion to guide future exploration it is incredibly hard to reach, let alone maintain. Those rare individuals (and they are rare indeed), who reach the mountain peak of infinity without the guidance of a guru, often advocate a route of 'no route' for the achievement of liberation in others. Usually they have fallen into Transcendent Awareness because of their nearness to it in the achieving lifetime. This may well be coupled with an intense desire to escape the suffering of the physical and to live a different awareness. Their own spontaneous Self-realization leads them to teach others that meditation techniques, and gurus, are not a necessity for gaining enlightenment. But, the fact is that most people are a long way from achieving this state of awareness and they need both the purifying presence of one who knows Transcendence, and an effective technique to speed their own revelation. Those whom enlightened teachers instruct do not begin their search from the same level of awareness as their teacher and, as this wisdom will never be fully recognized until it is gained, describing it without the addition of a technique for going deeply within and experiencing it may create confusion. Describing presence with language is an impossibility; it is beyond words. Teaching that it is already there and all that is needed is to turn towards it is nebulous teaching. Furthermore it encourages the 'no effort is needed' school of thought. The Self-realized Krishnamurti taught (and I use this word loosely as he did not describe himself as a guru) that gurus and teachings were not called for to achieve inner liberation. He reached the greatest earthly spiritual achievement on his own and therefore took the view that others could too. But his followers were left wondering.

Of course, those who prescribe a route of 'no route' are, in reality, offering a kind of method, however vague. Krishnamurti advocated sitting in a quiet place and watching thoughts come and go. This was his method. But an ill-defined route does not offer the help that most people need. Krishnamurti, when he gained Self-realization, understood that Transcendence had always been there. His awareness had grown to the point where it was no longer clouded. His description of his experience of liberation, although helpful on one level, was no easy means by which others could achieve it for themselves. This search will be made simple if a Transcendent intermediary is used to create the vibration of presence, now and mindfulness during meditation.

~ Healing the World ~

Something I have often heard from many types of healer is that they are here to heal the world; manifested in a way which implies their incarnation has nothing to do with their own healing or development. In fact, a spiritual healer's priority, like anybody else, must be to become Self-realized. If spiritual healers assist others towards enlightenment that is wonderful, but the real healing of others will come from the healer's own personal achievement of self-purification. Then, when established in inner peace, the healer's vibration is raised to the level of stillness and this will radiate to those around them. Those it touches will be encouraged, even if unconsciously, to purify themselves. This is the darshan of the enlightened. The spiritual healer will automatically illumine those who come into contact with them. The world is a reflection of the quality of its consciousness and the intensity of its suffering will mirror this. The world's healing will be a result of its awakening. The ultimate healing act is to spread the highest light through the earth by using Transcendent techniques and the seeking of Avataristic Grace. The more purity of Awareness there is in society, the greater support there will be for less damaging, more spiritually evolutionary decisions. Politicians whose decisions are governed by the collective awareness will respond to a purer atmosphere. It is in this way the children of the world will be helped, not only through outer means, but through the support of a purifying Transcendent vibration. In addition to their physical responsibilities for children the most a guardian can do is to assist the children in their care to achieve spiritually, and for the guardian or parent to heighten their own awareness. A family member slipping into enlightenment will lighten the vibrations of other family members for numerous past and future incarnations. If this were to happen there would be a greater cascading of wisdom. The animal kingdom, another reflection of consciousness, would also be healed through this. It is through a Transcendent intermediary for healing and their own enlightenment that spiritual healers will begin to heal the world.

~ Readiness ~

'Readiness' is another common New-Age refrain. Many are the times I have heard the expression "I am not ready". Anyone who says that they are not ready for something is unconsciously attempting to abdicate from responsibility for their choice. When I was first involved in spiritual healing events I used to watch people pick up books, look at them, pronounce them valuable, and then declare themselves "not ready to read that yet". They were making a choice not to look more deeply at something which might have expanded their understanding. Each incarnation an individual has is the opportunity to integrate more

Transcendence. The ramifications of their previous thoughts and actions, and the resultant patterns of behavior, will determine the type of choices that present themselves. This may on occasions appear restricting. *But, if an opportunity to develop spiritually is presented to them that individual is ready.* Each time a person declares themselves unready they will reduce their possibilities further and those who are attempting to introduce this wisdom will have to try harder. A general belief in 'unreadiness' will make more work for the Avatars and teachers.

A teacher of spiritual healing in a large organization once told me that the people who came to her to learn the visualization and channeling techniques she taught were "not ready" to practice Transcendent healing techniques. Her judgment was not based on an objective foundation of Transcendent Awareness; she stated she had had no revealing experiences of this. I felt in the course of the conversation she knew that there was an opportunity and choice for her: to find out more about the process of achieving higher states of consciousness, or to dismiss what I was saying. But her identification and status as a tutor of spiritual healing was in jeopardy. If she decided to take a fast spiritually developing route, whatever that route was, she would have to drop her belief that both she and the people she was tutoring were not ready to evolve. In the event she decided to cling more tightly to the illusory identity of tutor she had created for herself. She rejected what I was saying and insisted that her pupils were "not ready". I am sure these sorts of rationalizations are not made consciously, nevertheless they involve a choice. To justify her choice and attachment to an identity, the rationalization of non-readiness was made. It is true that only when a searcher of knowledge is 'ripe' will they become established in Transcendence, but there is never a time of having to be ready to start this journey. *There is no time in the future to start this venture, no right date, there is only now.* How can anyone have to be ready to know what they already are? This wisdom is available now should the choice be made to turn towards it. Clinging to any created identity and form is equivalent to a choice being made to deny oneself this opportunity.

~ Resonance ~

The advice I have seen most often given to new members at spiritual healing events is to "take what resonates". They are told to discard anything they hear that does not resonate with them. But if something which is truth does not resonate with an individual, where does that leave them? It can leave them only in one place and that is in ignorance of truth. There may be many ways of searching but there is only one truth. Believing themselves able to ignore truth, because it does not fit with their present worldview, is to deny themselves liberation. It is important to understand what spiritual development really is and to stop and question. If the help that is being refused is likely to assist in the achievement of expanded consciousness, then it is vital to look again at what has been rejected.

~ New Energies Coming into the World ~

An assumption in the teaching of the New-Age movement, about the inevitability of the process of spiritual development, has reached the point where a general belief exists that effort is not necessary. This is now accepted thinking and is exemplified in the prevalent 'energies coming in' view. According to spiritual healers, the 'new energies' which are coming into the world will heal it. Certainly, any higher vibrations affecting the earth will raise the vibration of its inhabitants, but it is a mistake to think that individual longing is not necessary. These higher vibrations will need to be assimilated and it is essential that people become conscious of the process. *There are no energies coming into this earth which are not already at the core its inhabitants.* It is not these energies which will heal the world but the willingness to raise humanity's collective vibration. This will be achieved most effectively through the introduction of the highest vibration of all. Individual determination will be indispensible.

~ Manifestation ~

Currently one of the most popular New-Age activities is to learn to manifest. This is a result of an important development in understanding: that through thought we create. But as yet this activity appears to lack a spiritual foundation.

Someone I met at a mind-body-spirit event claimed to have manifested a large sum of money. The experience had left them reeling. They had realized that if they could manifest money, if there was a negative aspect within which they may not be aware of, then the result might be manifesting something undesirable. They understood what I am saying in this book, although they might not have expressed it in the same way. Their understanding was: what is manifested will accord with the degree of spirituality. Unless inner impulses are pure and aligned with the evolutionary impulse of Transcendence, what is manifested may not serve a spiritual purpose. Anything which is manifested, consciously or unconsciously, may be a distraction to spiritual progress. The very act of manifesting may be clutching. Only by taking awareness beyond thought to the Source of all manifestation will what is manifested be a conscious process and consistently have spiritual purpose.

~ To Conclude ~

The purpose of this book is to urge all whom it touches to take effective action, in particular for healers to begin to use a Transcendent intermediary. The avid interest in outer phenomena within the New-Age movement coupled with its fledgling status, plus what often I feel is complacency, will dissolve in the light of growth into Transcendence. From the point of view of Divine Awareness there is only behavior which is evolutionary or not. This 'play' of knowing density and light is the 'play' of our own ability to create diversity; a capacity which is a gift afforded to us from the Divine. Action, whether it is supportive of spiritual evolution or not, can provide a release from the pitfalls that have been created or it can bind an individual to them more strongly. Until Divine status is reached non-evolutionary decisions are always possible.

To say that one is not ready is to decide such. There is never a time of being ready to receive Divine Grace.

8

Variations Within Light

The New-Age movement speaks much of inner wisdom. It describes how we are all beings of choice and light. It refers to light as if it were constituted of one single vibration, always discriminating and wise. However, this is not the case: the discernment inherent within light ranges from physical to infinite. Light is not homogenous, hence there are many different 'light healings'. Choice is also a word that features highly in New-Age teaching. The received view is that everyone leads the life they do because of the choices they have made. But choices may be limited. The concept of trusting our inner wisdom is popular too but who is it that people trust if they do not know the director within; the inner observer and knower of themselves - their Transcendent essence? How can someone trust what they do not know? A belief in New-Age teachings of inner wisdom only holds value if that is absorbed and maintained as a living experience not just as an intellectual understanding. There is nothing inherently incorrect about these views on inner wisdom; but the laissez-faire approach, the all-encompassing teachings that have been adopted, have allowed a multitude of ineffective, and at times non-evolutionary practices, to pronounce themselves as methods of spiritual liberation. From an evolutionary perspective it is pointless for the New-Age movement to constantly echo refrains such as "we are all creatures of compassion, light, choice and unconditional love who create our own reality" when its practices lack coherent, effective, fast techniques for reaching and *living* this knowledge. The New-Age movement accepts that people are unconscious but nevertheless appears content for them to remain in ignorance; it is seemingly at ease with this. Many are the articles I have read in which those who do speak of their experience of higher states of awareness also suggest that it is a once in a lifetime experience, one that cannot be maintained while on earth but only in a different dimension. The challenge now for members of the maturing New-Age is to move away from an identification with an anything-goes liberalism and begin to introduce the consistent wisdom of a consciousness-first teaching.

The most important attribute in life is spiritual wisdom and the discernment it brings. Spiritual discernment is the ability to understand behavior and its spiritual content or otherwise. At the basis of all understanding is an expanded, or limited, faculty of spiritual discernment. Its presence will depend on the expansion of awareness in both the individual and the collective. The teaching on choice (that all individuals are fully responsible for the lives they lead) does not take into consideration the present spiritual climate, a climate which is without the presence of an expanded faculty for spiritual discernment, where most responses are made unconsciously. A better description for this type of choice is 'habitual reactions'. These habits might come from impulses which emanate from deeply held, subconscious emotions and desires. In other words our hidden motives result in our patterns of being. This is not real choice. These patterns will be deep and dormant, awaiting their triggers. When activated old conduct may surface. The triggers present a person with the opportunity to exhibit the same behavioral pattern as before and so compound it. Simultaneously they provide the opportunity to change their response. With subtlety, latent motives create avenues for their expression, these will appear completely rational on the physical level. The outer justification given for responses may be very different to the inner original motive of the hidden impulse. Covertly instigated, the playground in which past impressions are addressed is formed. Non-evolutionary behavior may even be seen as spiritual under this guise. It is only one with spiritual discernment who will fully penetrate the facade of the action. Rarely are the motives which are given for behavior solely the reasons proffered. It is based on the predominance of subliminal impulses. The conduct of a society is also governed by the consciousness of the collective and its deeply held communal patterns. These consistently resurface and incite old conflicts. There is also the painful pattern of collective purification through natural disasters.

The most precious moments of our lives are those we spend in deep communion with Transcendence. The purification and transmutation this facilitates allows a pure, wise vibration of light to be incorporated into awareness. Wise light creates clarity and insight and an ability to see beyond the physical. The non-evolutionary vibrations incorporated within denser light are unable to hide in the presence of one with a high vibration. When living life with the purest light vibration in awareness, not only can the surface reasoning someone gives for their action be seen but, if necessary, inner unconscious motives will be visible (there were examples of this in Chapter 7 in the section on life aspects). If desired, the higher spiritual purpose of events will be understood. Similarly the motives of one who acts from a wise, pure light perspective may be very different from the assumed, often misunderstood, motives others may attribute to them. Spiritual development may sometimes be perceived as arrogance but more often than not arrogance and overconfidence is mistaken for spiritual development. The narrower vision of one without Transcendence in perception may easily be convinced by a confident, yet false, guru. One who lives with the dual perspective of outer reactive light and Transcendence will act spontaneously from that spiritually discriminating level of wisdom.

"You can take a horse to water but you can't make it drink." Never was there a more apt expression when referring to healing. Once, during meditation, I saw a vision of hell. The sights and sounds were horrendous: a land full of groups of people with their hands reaching upwards from the darkness crying out for help, ragged bandaged bodies crawling along the floor. Suddenly Jesus appeared and walked through the scene leaving a trail of blazing light in his wake. The teaching: that light in the world brings spiritual choice and the purer the vibration of light the more helpful it is for choices and responses which support spiritual evolution. The light of the Avatar and their Transcendent teachings always provide such a spiritually supportive choice no matter when or where they appear. The opportunity to take a different option and to respond to a situation in an evolutionary way lies within the connecting point of stillness, which is Transcendence and its pure vibration. It is this which is between an experience and the response to it. Waking in the morning a moment of Pure Awareness might be experienced, before the memories of yesterday and the days and years before it flood into the mind. This is individual awareness passing through the connecting point even when it is not yet firmly established. This is the still space between the sleeping and waking states of consciousness. Transcendent Awareness exists between every state of consciousness, waking, dreaming and sleeping, and is between each thought and breath. It is more easily accessible at these connecting points, and integrating awareness of this stillness and light is more usually achieved between the other transitional states of living and dying. In a less spiritually conscious condition responses do not incorporate an awareness of this still space, of the gap between events and responses to them. The result of this is a habitual response which comes from holding tightly to familiar patterns of behavior. Animals exhibit this state clearly; without the faculty of expanded choices they act predominantly on instinct. As human beings we have the capacity to widen our experience of this connecting space. If we immerse ourselves in a pure wise light vibration and incorporate an expanded perception with

Transcendence, from where spiritual wisdom and discernment emanate, a greater potential for spiritually evolutionary responses is created. Transcendent systems, as opposed to other techniques, introduce into the healing and meditation *directly and constantly* the purest wisdom. Then a more supportive platform on which to base decisions is awakened within. It is regularly cultivating awareness of the still space of Transcendence which breaks the cycle of habitual action because it offers Grace in the form of transmutation. This is a consciousness-first practice. With this integration and liberation the triggers of old habitual responses fail to arouse the same reactions. This expansion of consciousness may also have benefits for a person's physical well-being. The Transcendent presence and blessing of the Avatar also bring this same Grace; this can be with or without consciousness of the process.

The Grace of Mother Divine

I was on the train traveling to see a physical aspect of Mother Divine. A commuter boarded, seating herself halfway down the carriage. She was a woman, but it was extremely difficult to tell her sex so marred was her appearance. Her face was completely disfigured, so much so that the features were hardly visible; her hands were also totally scarred. I felt so sorry for her and wondered how she coped carrying such outer difference. Later in the day, when in the very close presence of Mother Divine, I asked her to heal this woman.

The next morning I went back to the same venue. I had been due to travel earlier but had missed my first train and also my connection. The connecting train I caught was extremely busy, but again I saw the badly disfigured person. As the train came to a halt and the carriage quickly filled up I wondered if she might sit nearby. Nevertheless I was amazed when the only free seat was taken by this woman and it was opposite me. She started to chat, complaining about the fact that the train was always so full and how unfair it was that there was a first-class carriage which remained half empty. After a while she turned to reading her newspaper and again, inwardly, I asked Mother Divine to heal her. As I did so I saw a layer of dark energy appear from deep within the woman. It slowly rose up her body and hovered above her head, eventually leaving her completely. In the dense vibration that lifted upwards I saw her as a young Indian woman. Her face had been intentionally scarred, she had been cast out by her family and was lying on the floor being belittled by onlookers. I do not know into which caste she had been born in that life, but what she became in the eyes of those around her, because of her disfigurement and consequent unsuitability for marriage, was untouchable. She became a beggar and spent the rest of her life suffering abject poverty, stigmatization and total rejection. Being deliberately scarred and considered the lowest of the low, and holding the pain from this experience, had induced her present physical characteristics. It had also instigated her resentment of those whom she felt were not deserving of special, first-class status. The train pulled into a station and I stood up to get off. Lost in my thoughts I mistakenly believed that I had arrived at my destination. As I continued the last part of the journey standing by the door I realized that this woman's perception of the situation would have been very different from my reality. She would have thought that I had preferred to travel standing up away from her, fueling her belief that others were repulsed by her physical form and she was indeed undesirable. Such a view would have reinforced her own painful pattern and so her reality. I saw, however, the source of this distress so clearly removed from her physical system that I was sure any future incarnation would not be blighted so overwhelmingly by such stigma.

Such is the nature of a consciousness-first healing. Subconscious acquiescence and evolutionary support showed when the only seat available was opposite and claimed by this woman. It did not change her physical appearance in this lifetime, but had, in spite of this,

> *begun to release her from her deep holding of this reality: impressions formed from retaining emotional responses to her past. The intermediary of Transcendence does not need to analyze the trauma of the past. Its innate wisdom and evolutionary impulses ensure an inner-to-outer approach, Grace in the form of transmutation facilitating a greater and more permanent possibility for change. Unconsciously this woman had been liberated from future suffering.*

Choice is a facet of a certain state of evolution, as is the existence of the human mind with its communication and analyzing processes. Go deeper into evolution and it is possible to see that all human choices and responses can be brought into consciousness. Transcendence, beyond thought, is what their connecting stillness is made up of. Integrating and maintaining awareness of this discerning space, so it is present during routine activity, is the process of spiritual development and gaining the light of inner wisdom.

I am not suggesting that the transmutation of karma is never reached through other non-Transcendent sorts of healing. It can take place if the light of the healer and receiver of the healing is such that purer light vibrations are generated between them. But this is much more difficult to achieve without a system which ensures a constant link to Transcendence. Many New-Age practices, despite their claims, do not introduce the necessary transmuting vibration. Some prefer the route of devotional practice. This also has the potential to work but needs to be practiced with great intensity. An outer display of devotion has to be a reflection of deep inner faith. If true devotion is lacking, nothing more than an attachment to ritual is the result. There has to be an inner deep openness for accepting Grace. Inner devotional intensity is based on previous experience. With no prior clear sense of the Divine to sustain and direct it, maintaining a deep faith (the pathway of devotion) can be erratic and difficult to sustain. The pathway of the system therefore becomes the option that most seekers choose. If a person alone does not have or is unable to reach such intense experience, both the Avatar and the Transcendent system will help them to attain it:

- Love of the Avatar stirs yearning and devotion.
- The joy and benefits of a meditation experience which is immersion in stillness creates a desire for more.
- This results in a greater determination for regular experience.
- The result of this is life-enhancing; it fills the meditator with aspiration and a subsequent affection for what they are experiencing.

It is at this point that the pathways of the system and devotion become one, resulting in an amalgamation of persistence and discipline with appreciation and love. In this way the Transcendent system and the Avatar fulfill the same function; when individuals are unable to reach the Divine on their own, both are able to help. Such development involves a growth of the heart but the heart will not develop fully until the mind has gained an understanding of infinity. In Patanjali's[1] compilation of teachings he says:

> And when the translucent intellect is as pure as the Self, there is Enlightenment.

Many spiritual healing trainers encourage visualizing the expansion of the heart in the belief that discrimination and wise behavior come from it, rather than from the mind. But an intelligent heart is the *fruit* of enlightenment. From the first stage of enlightenment the heart will begin to expand with devotion as a *result* of the joy from what its senses, mind and intellect perceive. A consciousness-first approach will make this possibility easy. This spontaneous opening of the heart is the opposite of using the force of visualization; as already seen this is a process full of uncertainty as an undeveloped heart may attract unwanted negativity. A heart which is opened prematurely in a non-evolved state is vulnerable to attracting less helpful influences (this point has already been made in Chapter 7). The heart will only safely expand and develop when the senses are able to perceive what is truly at the basis of physical existence (the experience of this is described in Chapter 11). Judgments and choices made, either with mind or heart, will reflect an individual's spiritual wisdom and discernment. The free will that they use to make decisions today, consciously or not, will create the band of options that present themselves in the future.

It is time for the New-Age movement to come of age and develop more insight and discrimination, time for its healers and recipients to begin to assess the multifaceted practices that are at its core. It is important that this is done on a basis of the consciousness-first and wise-light content of its therapies. Anything which pushes awareness towards Transcendence is a help and is a healing. However, raising understanding of healing to become an act which emanates solely from a deep change of awareness, one which incorporates totality into individual consciousness, would be an evolutionary step, for both individuals and the collective consciousness of the world. The vibration of infinity restructures an individual's physical form with discernment and power and is therefore more effective. If a greater collective spiritual awareness were the reality not only would an individual's possibilities become less painful, due to a release from their behavioral patterns, there would also be more societal support for spirituality. This would be the outcome of a pure vibration of light generated in the collective, supporting real choices to make different responses on both an individual and group level. Dense reactive light can only be safely and successfully persuaded to display itself, and be transmuted, by the wisdom and Grace of pure eternal light. This ensures that physical benefits really do reflect an expansion of consciousness. It is the responsibility of the New-Age movement to encourage not just physical but spiritually transforming practices through the incorporation of Transcendence; nothing compares with its power.

The light of the Transcendent shines like a beacon. It is not the outer light of the physical universe nor of any physical being which resides within it. These are its reflections.

9

Wise Healing

During a healing I am aware of the vibration I use, I see it emanating from total stillness, both within me and the person I am healing. Once, when in America studying to become an Authorized Instructor of The Second Degree of The Radiance Technique®, this spontaneous display remained in my perception for days. Understanding how spiritual healings can be raised to create this sounder connection to Transcendence (or the Divine Source as it is often called on spiritual healing courses) requires clear insight into the process of healing. It is a Transcendent connection which ensures that healing emanates from a place of real compassion and unconditional love, as opposed to any other human emotion. When I talk of spiritual healing generally I am also including the reiki practices I have come across. Of the numerous reiki practitioners I have met, including those who call themselves reiki 'masters', each technique they used differed. Many of these reiki practitioners were clearly, although unknowingly, using spiritual healing visualization techniques similar to those taught by spiritual healing organizations. The reiki healers who were not practicing spiritual healing visualizations, and activated their healing by using what they all called 'cosmic symbols', also employed a multitude of methods. I have seen endlessly differing reiki healings which involved completely distinct creations they called attunements. The reiki healers I have taught underwent a variety of different attunement procedures from their numerous teachers (all of whom who were purporting to be teaching the authentic system). As I said in Chapter 1, I have yet to come across a technique that is just called reiki which I personally feel creates a direct and constant connection to Transcendence. The same is true for the many spiritual healings I have observed. The result is a reactive, outer, physical vibration being the intermediary for healing. Among spiritual healers, irrespective of what they do with the denser energy they remove, their unifying action is the use of their physical bodies as 'channels for the Divine'. In spiritual healing circles this would be done consciously; in a non-Transcendent reiki healing it usually happens unconsciously. Lacking the protection that a pure vibration offers leaves these healers, no matter what name they give themselves, open to the energy of both the person they are healing and other outside influences.

When referring to spiritual healings my use of the plural is deliberate; in fact I would go so far as to say that there is no such thing as 'spiritual healing' only 'spiritual healings'. Contrary to current belief, healers' capabilities vary. Their individual vibrations reverberate quite differently. Much depends on the physical system of the healer as it is a meter of their level of spiritual awareness. This will affect the kind of healing they are able to perform. Their thoughts, and frequency of the vibration that lies behind them, reflect their degree of closeness to knowing Transcendent Awareness. Healings will vary widely. One of the first and most famous spiritual healers in the UK was Harry Edwards. He is still revered today for the healing work he did. Harry Edwards's conclusion on the healing process was that there had to be what he called a "form of thought application". Furthermore that the standard of a healer's personality played its part in the quality of the healing. Often spiritual healers reduce the significance of their role by saying, "I had nothing to do with it, it was the energy / spirit working through me". Harry Edwards, however, implied that when practicing spiritual healing it is never a "nothing to do with me" affair. If the quality of healing is affected by thoughts then it has everything to do with the healer and it is predominantly to do with their spiritual evolution. As indicated earlier, wisdom and spiritual discrimination are determined by this. Awareness is expressed through desires, emotions and intentions. From these come thoughts and action. The vibrations which underpin them may be conscious or not. The more spiritually evolved the individual, the greater the ability to access, without assistance and through their own physical being, a purer, wiser, more effectively transmuting vibration of light. As the body of the spiritual healer is the intermediary for healing, nothing they think or do is insignificant. Emotions, and intentions held during spiritual healing, no matter how deep or hidden, will have an affect on its outcome.

The ultimate aim of spiritual healers is to display a pure Transcendent light vibration through the medium of their own physical form. Spiritual healers, when attempting to attune to this Divine Source in order to channel it, turn their attention inwards to raise their own vibration in whatever way they know. They do this through invocation, meditation, visualizing light or a combination of these activities. By raising their own vibration the healer then displays a higher vibration to the person being healed. This encourages and assists the recipient to also focus their attention inwards, to raise and purify their own vibration and so to self-heal. Spiritual healing is therefore the display and effect of the vibration of the healer's own state of being, heightened as much as possible. In spiritual healing, as with other forms of healing, it is the interaction between two vibrations of light, that which the healer can access and the recipient's own, which constitutes the healing. Vitally, any inability of the healer to maintain a constant connection to Transcendence results in less support being offered to the person being healed. With the multitude of individual vibrations and combinations of vibrations being used there will inevitably be variations within healings. Some of these may encourage the recipient's awareness to take a positive direction, towards Transcendence and its transmuting Grace; others may not.

The following represents the physical body:

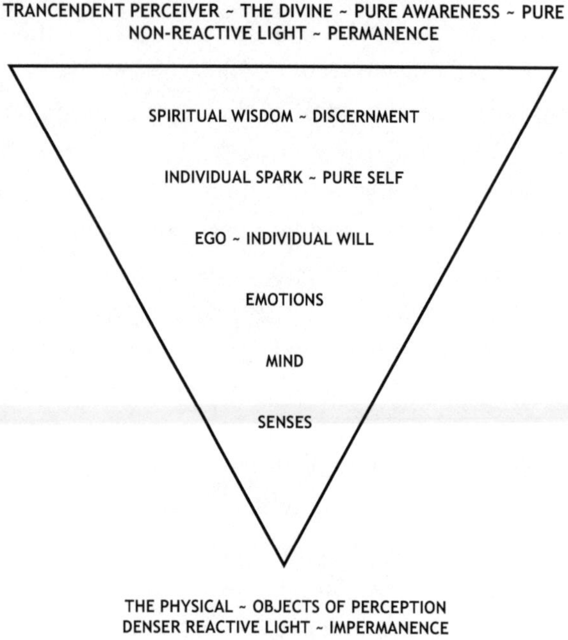

Through the senses we perceive, we know and experience the outer world. Information from the senses is registered by the mind but the mind does not act alone. The senses are also connected to the emotional level and the mind discriminates through both intellect and feeling. Behind the emotions lies the individual ego. How much a human ego has incorporated the evolutionary impulses of Transcendence depends upon the extensiveness of the individual's awareness. Beyond human ego lies an individual spark, the essence of a human's purest physical form. This was brought into being by the evolutionary desire of the Divine. Within the denser physical levels, the senses, mind and emotions, within all healers lie the different experiences, beliefs and habitual responses: the impressions and attachments formed from past and present lives. Different life aspects and their individuality are influential in the present life body. Many of the emotions and realities these personalities harbor lie dormant and hidden in the unconscious. There is much, then, for the spiritual healer to attune through; and the possibility of accessing a pure vibration will be affected by it. It is feasible that subliminal impulses could come to the foreground and predominate within the act of healing. It is because of the use of their own physical systems that there is a risk of an exchange of energy: the absorption of the recipient's vibrations by the healer or the depletion of the healer's own energy in favor of the person being healed. Then there is the extended possibility of other life aspects entering and attaching themselves, either to the healer or the client. The degree of protection the spiritual healer generates against outside influences, usually by visualizing light around themselves, will depend upon the quality of the light vibration they are able to invoke. The visualization of light is no guarantee of insulation from another's influence.

As suggested above, I believe that the outcome of all healing, no matter what form it takes, ultimately rests on the quality and collaboration of the light between the individuals involved. And, light used for healing may be anything but pure. The healing space created results in this interaction and determines the character of the choices presented. How the options offered are utilized will depend on the perception of the person being healed. Their reaction to the healing will usually be made unconsciously. Whether or not the light displayed by the intermediary of the spiritual healer alone is able to raise the vibration of the person receiving healing (enough to create for them a transmutation choice) is an uncertainty. When spiritual healing, or non-Transcendent reiki, takes place transmutation is most likely to be an option which is erratic and intermittent. No healing interferes with any individual's choice but, as with the story of the hypnotist, a vibration of light which contains hidden impulses can be influential, even dominating, and these may not always push towards evolution. Whether the possibilities available to the recipient of spiritual healing are spiritually evolutionary or not will vary. The range will be from: no change at all, to removing lower vibrations, but only providing some temporary distance and not transmuting them, to the choice of transmutation and so a change in individual consciousness. Should a direct, Transcendent vibration be used it would also resonate within the healer. At the same time as healing someone else it would offer the healer the same supreme choice of transmutation. The pure light of the infinite generates a vibration of a totally different quality to that of the diverse channeled light that spiritual healers use. It is beyond human emotions and intentions.

It is a mistake for spiritual healers to believe that, when unenlightened, they have the ability to display a pure and constant Transcendent vibration. It is only because the physical system of the Avatar is so pure that it constantly vibrates the highest healing power of Transcendence. Any spiritual healer able to maintain Transcendent Awareness throughout the whole of their healing session could only do so if they were already sustaining this outside their spiritual healing practice. Such a healer would be living in a state of enlightenment. Only in enlightenment are inner impulses pure and conscious. No healer, spiritual, reiki or otherwise, is a master of anything if they do not have the mastery that comes from living enlightenment. For any healer to give the most spiritually evolutionary, and therefore most beneficial, healing it is imperative that they access the highest vibration when healing others. For this to occur they will need to use the eternal vibration of Transcendence which will ensure that the efficacy of their healing is elevated beyond their own individual ability. Adding this capacity is not only for their clients' benefit, but for the healer's own personal protection and clarity of perception, both of which will be strengthened. In order to achieve an enhancement in their healing it is advisable for all healers to do two things:

- Use the vibration from Transcendent systems to meditate with regularly and seek the Grace of an Avatar – to develop spiritually and thereby raise their own vibration.

- Use a pure Transcendent intermediary – this will offer to those being healed the pure vibration of spiritual discernment and Grace. The quality of this consciousness-first approach will ensure that connecting points of stillness, transmutation and the possibility of integration of heightened awareness are made available. This is both for healer and client.

Healers of the New-Age movement must begin to offer their clients the most support possible. It is at the level of Transcendence alone, the Source of all light, that the outer physical reactive light of the body is effectively restructured.

The most praiseworthy aspiration of any healing is to ensure that, alongside the relief of physical symptoms, an opportunity for spiritual development is created. And as discussed, some healing is more effective than others. Offering this opportunity constitutes a true healing; a transformation in awareness through the incorporation of a vibration which is beyond the senses. This is the skill of healing, maintaining during the healing process a constant connection to Transcendence. I believe it is necessary for spiritual and reiki healers to look realistically at their healing practice, be honest, and see that most are not so intimate with the Divine Source that they can activate this transmuting process without help. In fact it is an impossibility unless the spiritual healer is living higher states of consciousness (described later in Chapter 11). If higher awareness is not present then the healing will benefit from the use of a Transcendent intermediary. Raising healing to this status, and enhancing the quality of this service to humanity, is every healer's challenge. Raising individual vibration to that of enlightened is everyone's. When realized in the healer, the wise healing which results is a healing free of all denser vibrational influence, a healing where the healer does not have to learn how to be protected but becomes one with the Source of protection: being one with the Source of all the impulses of spiritual evolution and gaining wise perception. This is becoming one with the Source of unconditional love which raises human love to the level of infinite and unconditional, a love with no boundaries or expectations. A healing might not necessarily result in a physical cure, although this may be a consequence of receiving it, offering a pure healing (and becoming healed) is achieving this connection to Source and gaining enlightenment. For this last realization all will need the help of the Avatar. It is not enough, however, to rely on the purity of the Avatar for liberation and not make an equivalent individual effort. The least exertion anyone can make is to access Transcendence daily. It is also necessary to beware of teachers with a strong, determined and influential vibration who may appear knowledgeable but are not in touch with their own Transcendent nature: to ask if they are awake and *living* the states of awareness I will describe and if they are not, to find one who is: to be aware of teachers and teachings which enhance individual ego. Healers abound who tell their clients what they would like to hear. Being told that the most beautiful angel is their constant, hidden companion, or that their energy feels "good", true or otherwise, is every searcher's dream. Being told that humility and determination are essential for spiritual development is less easy to accept. Understanding that many teachers and teachings are described as enlightened and transmuting when they are not is paramount. They will be of little benefit to the true seeker.

The further away from Transcendence the less power is available. This is true of both individuals and the teachings and the practices they use. The skill in healing is to discriminate. To know the difference between those systems which are evolutionary and consequently of greater spiritual help, and those which are less so. This is a faculty that until now only few have developed. Our present world reflects the amount of spiritual wisdom that collectively humanity has allowed to flow through it. All healers could now learn about their ability to work with Transcendence, understand how to place its vibration in the physical world, and so awaken further the possibilities for humankind. In 1978 I studied some advanced meditation techniques; they were taught directly by Maharishi. After the last of the courses, which took most of a year to complete, any willing course participants were flown to Iran. It was the time of the fall of the Shah and Maharishi was sending his army of light to meditate in that country. In doing this they emanated the vibration of Transcendence into the physical atmosphere and raised the collective vibration of that area. A similar project emerged within the TM movement at the time of the fall of the Berlin Wall where Maharishi's transcendental meditators surrounded the relevant areas of that city. A direct Transcendent vibration will emanate into the whole of the collective. In order to try and create effective and fast change in that area Maharishi had arranged for meditators to move to Berlin for this vibration to be felt more immediately. He claimed that the effect of 1% of transcendental meditators within a particular area would facilitate a positive change in the behavior of the residents. Evidence collected at the time appeared to support this view. Today it is no longer necessary to visit places in order to facilitate such change. Human awareness has developed to the point where, on a large scale, it can now incorporate a Transcendent light vibration into the world more simply. Hands which vibrate Transcendence, whenever they touch anything living, are a possibility for all healers and meditators. This is a huge advancement. It is achievable for all healers and meditators to learn Transcendent techniques which 'sew' this vibration into the fabric of the physical and anchor it into events, past, present and future. In doing this a greater awakening of the world will occur. This work can begin in spite of any lack of collective or individual enlightenment. It is this new application of spiritual power which will facilitate the next major transformation in human awareness. The Avatars and Transcendent systems which appear will reflect this burgeoning capability. Only if the Divine personalities and systems chosen are authentic, complete and pure, will this unfolding in individual and collective consciousness take place. The recognition of Transcendence as an intermediary will be an imperative. There must now be an understanding, even if only on an intellectual level, of the difference between the light vibration of Transcendence and physical reactive light. Using any vibration which is less than a direct emanation from totality will not instigate this major leap. Such an advancement will necessitate a consciousness-first approach.

Your only guide is the wisdom of your own perception.

From The Beatles to Brahman ~ Personal Experience of the Goal

10

Past-Life Continuum

From my youth I could see images of my past existence. I did not know the details, but very often pictures would float into my mind of me dressed in clothes I either did not recognize or I associated with other nationalities. I would know when I was rethinking and re-experiencing past emotions and thoughts. Later in these scenarios I began to see other people too. The images became startlingly clear early in 1993 when visions during meditation of my past, present and future began to unfold. One of the first of these was the face of an enlightened being who had been my father in a previous life. As I sat in meditation I watched myself back in India taking a stroll along the waterside with my father of the time. He had been both my guardian and my spiritual teacher. I did not pursue further information, did not ask questions or receive answers. I ignored much of it and again sought in meditation the silence that was the real teaching and these scenes ceased.

Later, some years ago, a friend introduced me to a past-life therapist that she trusted. I went to see them too because I was curious, nothing more. The method was visualization and a form of spiritual healing which invoked angelic forces. They spoke to the subconscious of the client in order to ascertain past experience, its teaching, and the client's held patterns. I felt totally at ease with this therapist and believed we had experienced a past-life relationship of some kind. I had only seen them a few times when they told me that I could do on my own what they were facilitating. For a while I followed the visualization instructions; later all I had to do was ask and film-like images of the past, and sometimes future, would open up in front of me.

The therapist's first statement to me was that their job was to help me know who and what I was. It was a joint project and 10 years later, although there were few physical meetings between us, this task was completed. Together we had relived the shadows of a past life. I have done many of the things that I am suggesting risk delaying spiritual progress and it was great fun. Eventually I became bored with uncovering past lives and it was at that time I began to wonder what people who did not have the liberating techniques of Transcendence were gaining from these visualizations. More importantly, what was being done to relinquish the retention of past pain (pain which was frequently more acute during these sessions)? It goes without saying that all the Transcendent skills I had at my fingertips were utilized to facilitate a healing release from my held patterns of pain. I knew, though, that this happened anyway when I just meditated with this vibration. My question again was: What was happening for people when this was not the case? Certainly there is an intellectual understanding of the past lives to be gained. But how could the therapist ensure they were analyzing the source of the problem and be certain that a healing which was not Transcendent reached all the client's life aspects? I was aware that past-life personalities did not always present themselves immediately. I asked myself what was really happening if there was no transmuting vibration brought to the events under scrutiny. I had reached the conclusion that if the combined physical light of the therapist and client was such that it introduced a higher vibration of light (and therefore greater spiritual discernment), then some potential was created for an evolutionary push towards Transcendence. But, if the combined physical light of the therapist and client did not create that opportunity, what was actually happening? I believe that the therapist I saw had more wisdom and light than most. But I have since met many past-life therapists and clients so desiring of information about their previous lives that this process has become not their pathway to liberation, but their stumbling block. Many times I hear statements such as "it comes from a past life" as a response to circumstances and difficulties. The problem for the client, however, has presented itself not solely because of their past experience and conduct (as in crime and punishment and good deeds and rewards) but because a pain is being held onto and carried into the present form. From an enlightened perspective an attachment to form is nothing more than an identification with a created illusion. Clinging to the physical expressed through "I am" is just as much an identity with form when it becomes "I was".

I ceased looking at my past lives; the effectiveness of the techniques I possessed was releasing me from the habitual patterns and pain of these without the need for an intellectual understanding. Then, in 2002, I began to suffer what turned out to be a minor but persistent physical problem. I needed a doctor for the first time in 15 years and therefore, because of my nature, I was determined to know why (without such a strong desire this book could not have been written). I had once been told, by a psychic that I trusted at the time, that I would be "shaken up" in order to know my true nature. Middle-age was when this occurred. According to Ayurvedic medicine the menopause is the time for a woman when what is unresolved may surface. What women do about this is individual, but for me, it was an unstoppable push from the Divine which led to me understanding my part in the collective story. I realized afterwards, when I could see all sides of events, that the fire and passion within me, normally associated with youth and direction, had been suppressed. Until this point there had been nothing in my life except spiritual development which had captured my enthusiasm. I had been content to concentrate solely on an inner investigation at the expense of outer interests. This unused potential became reignited and pushed into my awareness. It was a time of upheaval, exhaustion and a huge broadening of perception. It was not comfortable; the symptoms and events made more dramatic and forceful in order to overcome my resistance. The necessity of healing led to an inner focus which at any other time I would have thought obsessive and unhelpful. But I began to perceive with a vision which was becoming liberated from the impressions of the past. At the same time as undergoing mid-life symptoms the attitude of someone close began to change towards me, deepening the upheaval and distress. I observed that my clinging to painful patterns of behavior had caused an eruption of the same circumstances in my present life. It was because of this enquiry that I realized that as well as warning me about the hurt still remaining to be dissolved, there had been one main purpose in the help the past-life therapist had given me. This was to encourage me to trust myself when I began spontaneously seeing past-life scenes and, more importantly, their connection to present events and my role. In the past, when confronted, I had not trusted myself. An increased spiritual awareness correlated with help that supported evolutionary impulses. This time my change of consciousness had led me to the therapist before the events occurred, unlike in previous lives. This was coupled with my willingness to prepare to change an old response which emanated from the experience of being thwarted when speaking out. The past-life pain I had felt made its presence felt again in the form of difficult symptoms. The hermit in the forest was being shaken up and an awareness of a duty reawakened. This time of change stirred up in my physical form what had been reflected and spoken of in my Jyotish life-chart: the push and pull of two opposing planets, one of extreme heat and one of extreme cold. The Jyotish life-chart representation was a mirror of two lines of pain. One reflecting a life where I had been cast out into the cold for speaking the same truth I am speaking in this book; the other, a life in which I had been burned for the same expression. Not until these lives started to heal did the drama of the symptoms begin to subside. The Jyotish life-chart depicted this too by showing evolutionary support for a different type of life-path. A life-path symbolic of a life I once had as an Indian woman who always wore a turquoise sari, a teacher of spirituality. The expansion of awareness which was emerging made the hermit stir and question the choice of isolation.

My vision was expanding to incorporate the overlap and connections of previous lives (mine and other people's) and to integrate an awareness of the continuum within what is usually perceived of as past and present. I could physically see this on the earth plane and perceive these life-layers. The past-life personalities within individuals were visible to me, displaying the same emotions and behavior the present personalities were showing. What I saw was painful and detailed and would be difficult to relate here. When I first started to have psychic vision, rarely was it as pictures in my mind. More often than not I saw the characters move and speak, as noted earlier, as though projected in a movie. This changed to become a genuine seeing. Many 'spiritual leaps' over the years, during which I would be suddenly aware of an increase in light and vibration within, had facilitated this vision. By the end of this turbulent mid-life experience I was actually seeing past-life personalities formed as shadows behind the present ones. When the third eye is truly open, seeing and knowing is no longer in the realm of intuition; it *really* does see. Angels and life aspects are there, a concrete part of reality, albeit a finer vibration of it. This way of perceiving increased over time and I also understood, not just with my mind but from awareness, that I was re-experiencing pain in this life because I had not taken the evolutionary decisions through which I could have avoided it. I also learned that the collective consciousness was relevant. A past scenario had been recreated. It was the same story and the same cast, the same spiritual tests. The result of all these dramatic spiritual jumps was that I started to see with a clarity and detail that had not occurred previously. My discernment had expanded in accordance with the increase of my awareness and it spontaneously began to include the connection of present life events to past lives. Decisions that were taken by individuals within these past lives revealed themselves as the source of much of their present experience. At each stage every understanding I experienced was real. But there are hidden depths to knowing and seeing. Above all this change taught me three things, two of which have already been discussed. Again not on an intellectual level but from a more penetrating awareness:

- Firstly: that present-day events trigger hidden emotions within people that would never be obvious or come to light in different circumstances. These emotions and response patterns lie dormant, waiting in the wings for the karmic event which will reignite them and present a spiritual test. They are embodied in past-life personalities.

- Secondly: that with more evolution, and a different response from a purer consciousness, less suffering would have been the outcome. I saw the two stories: the one that was, and the one that could have been based on a broader and sharper awareness. Karma is not simply something outside an individual which is unavoidable (although there may be times when it cannot be evaded). What a person does, in every minute of the day in the arena of outer reactive light, is the creation of their karma. Importantly, present thoughts, emotions and responses will shape the kind of impact karmic events have. Like the spider weaving its web it is the trap individuals weave for themselves. It is their stress. The effects of a returning karma on someone who has not evolved spiritually may be felt strongly and permanently. For someone who evolves further it may be painful and stay, but after time has passed the effects disappear. With more spiritual expansion its results are there for a time only to fade quickly. For the highest evolution there is little impact. Like using a pencil to draw on air it leaves no physical impression at all. Therefore no residual emotions or motives are left which prompt habitual behavior (these are the subconscious impulses spoken of in Chapter 8 which are given justification in the physical arena). In other words my mid-life pressure would have been less stressful had I evolved more.

- My third understanding: I recognized how differently the situation would have been in an age when the collective awareness was pure enough to support more spiritually supportive decisions, rather than those that had been made.

When I began to unravel my experience there was one person I felt I could talk to, but I had not seen them for 10 years and I believed them to be living abroad. The day after I had had this thought, during a conversation in which I did not mention the person in question, I was told that I could make contact as they were now living locally. Positive, evolutionary impulses also lie dormant in the unconscious, side by side with others; they too prompt an individual but they will support a move towards spiritually enhancing action. In 1978 I gave up a job that held little interest for me. I had been offered free accommodation and went to Scarborough with the intention of staying there for only a few weeks. The first people I met told me that the preparation courses for advanced meditation study were being held there, one of the first places in the country to offer them. I had no idea prior to arriving that these courses existed. I stayed and spent the best part of a year completing them all. I unconsciously walked into a space and time of huge personal evolution. When an individual's awareness is aligned with the support of

Transcendence they will find themselves in the right place and time for greater spiritual development. Often these supportive impulses are on a conscious level; certainly in a fully developed state every move, although still spontaneous, is consciously understood in terms of its evolutionary value. With this sort of awareness and assistance life flows much more smoothly. There is always some distress in this dense physical world, but in an enlightened state, alongside it, there is Transcendence and inner freedom. It is on the level of the mind that suffering is recognized and empathized with.

What those concerned in my mid-life story did was to create an arena where there was a legitimate rationalization for expressing inner non–evolutionary, probably unconscious, impulses. They allowed their dormant past personalities to emerge and express old behavioral responses. Their motives were not as they appeared on the surface. The event too, as such events always do, gave them the opportunity of testing and changing their subconscious patterns by offering the choice of reacting differently. But there is no guarantee that the opportunity for change will be utilized, and indeed displaying the same responses may compound the impressions they leave. If significant spiritual progress is not made, there is also the chance that even when behaving differently new patterns and habits may be created, new emotional pain and trauma held onto, and so a new habitual response created. This results in cycles of permanent pain.

Reinvoked Emotions

With healers I have witnessed behavior such as that displayed in past religious inquisitions and witch hunts, albeit on a much less physically damaging scale. Both those who were considered witches, and those who purged society of the heresy of these 'witches', believed themselves to be the healers of the day. These 'healers', in past eras, 'purged' by burning and hanging. In the name of purification they tortured and killed. Still today there is much potential for the detrimental strengthening of ego within the healing arena, for behavior which is based on fear, anger and arrogance. All over the world it is still possible to see inappropriate and often atrocious conduct, justified as if it emanated from a greater connection to the Divine, when clearly it does not. The resurgence of such events are contained and made less damaging because of evolution, both of the individual and the collective in which the individual finds themself, yet still these negative impulses seek expression.

After an event when held emotions and responses prompted a display of inappropriate, inquisitional behavior, a healer approached me to apologize. I explained to them my understanding of the higher spiritual purpose behind the emergence of the event and how I felt a spiritual test had been triggered by the retention of negative past-life emotions. They began to understand it for themselves, saying they could see that the individuals concerned had behaved in the same way as before. Although I had hardly spoken to this person before, I told them that should they not take this opportunity to evolve spiritually, a similar spiritual test and choice would present itself to them again. Most probably this would be in a future incarnation. As I spoke I astonished myself by speaking this way. It was as though an inner wakefulness watched as the words came from the deepest, purest, timeless part of me. Later that night, unable to sleep, a clear past-life scene opened up in front of me, as if watching a film at the cinema. It was a more detailed story of the past life with the witch-hunters and its residual impressions which had re-emerged in their behavior that day. I saw vividly that in this previous life, I engaged in exactly the same conversation as I had just had in this life, with the same individual who had just apologized. I had in the past life been pilloried, publicly ridiculed and beaten while awaiting hanging. At dead of night, for fear of attracting the anger of their colleagues, this person had brought me water. They apologized for their behavior. I told them then that they were experiencing an opportunity for spiritual development and liberation, that if they chose not to expand their awareness they would again be presented with this possibility, probably in a future incarnation. And the compassion of the Avatars and teachers would draw them back to the world to teach them once more about Transcendence. Furthermore, that precious physical time was being lost.

Like a record stuck in the groove, from their habit of holding onto emotions and patterns of responding, individuals cause distress to themselves and others. They act out the same habitual behavior. Until they make the choice to change, become aware of Transcendence and liberate themselves from their patterns, they will continue to incarnate and be presented with spiritual tests. Until they alter they will continue to suffer.

The sort of constraints that exist within society, the ways in which people are permitted to act, whether a society legitimates or sanctions behavior, will be representative of the collective spiritual awareness and the Grace it has received. The legal system reflects this. It is due to an increase in spirituality and Grace that our society no longer hangs and burns people considered to be witches. The way they are dealt with by the collective when their individual acts breach society's regulations changes over time; laws alter in response to the flow of consciousness. The collective awareness of each society will determine what is undesirable conduct and how much of it individuals are legally and morally permitted to display. This underlying control also works on more subtle levels of vibration; when more spiritual opportunities for an individual's negative impulses to emerge are negated. The awareness of each individual will determine the impact of events on them personally. The scenarios we find ourselves in are often the result of reliving the past and being overshadowed by past emotions which find their re-expression. This will continue until a different response point of Transcendence is created.

JJ's Healing

JJ came to see me for healing because she had a history of depression and binge-eating. These problematic habits had re-emerged after the death of her dog a few months earlier. JJ knew that she was in need of a big change, both in herself and her circumstances. I suggested, as I usually do, that at least three healing sessions as close together as possible would be the most beneficial and she agreed to this. I do not try to obtain psychic information when healing clients, preferring inner silence to psychic activity. It is not unusual, however, for me to see the life in which a problem began. I will often also inwardly see subsequent lives where the original difficulty was reignited, and compounded. I do not always feel it is helpful to speak about what I perceive as after all the problem is not in the past, but being experienced in the client's present physical form. I have seen the fascination that past-life stories hold for some people and the unhelpful way in which they are referred to; as if they were something beyond themselves. As a result, these lives become something beyond the sphere of personal responsibility and are blamed for current problems.

During the first of the three healings, with my inner vision I watched JJ in a prior existence. It was as though I was close, not participating but viewing. I saw JJ in a beautiful setting; she was rowing a boat on a lake, surrounded by mountains. Exactly where this was I am unsure but I felt it could be in what is now the French Alps, possibly around the 18th century. In the rowing boat was also a dog and a child: a curly-haired, blond little boy. I watched as the dog jumped into the lake, I saw also the child fall in after it. As I finished the healing I had a sense that JJ herself had ended up in the water and that all three of them may have died. I decided to speak about what I had seen and afterwards I told JJ that I had seen her on a beautiful lake, in a rowing boat with a child and a dog. I did not *tell her that I had felt that the boy had drowned and that she too had died. This was partly because I had wanted to wait until the next session to see what else unfolded, but also because I had had a sense that her depression had some connection with the loss (probably death) of a child. During this healing I also saw her in a different life scenario, holding lots of balloons, and was not sure what this image related to. I made a general comment that I had a feeling that the resurgence of her present emotions was something to do with a child. JJ then told me that she had suffered seven miscarriages and had not subsequently had children. (What she did tell me she saw during her healing was an Indian woman, dancing and dressed in a turquoise sari. I did not respond but this scene related to another life, a life of mine which I was already aware of. It appeared that JJ had been a part of this life too, but that is a different story.)*

As part of my role as a teacher of meditation in Cambridge I arrange opportunities for students to meet for group meditations and, as a group, we have in the past supported financially an orphanage and school in Cambodia. I had a very strong feeling after JJ's healing that it would be helpful for her to sponsor a child in the orphanage. This sponsorship could be arranged via a Cambodian charity, is structured and well-organized, and while there are regulations and limitations around the sponsoring process it does allow for a degree of physical contact between a child and their sponsor. It is possible for a relationship between them to develop. Despite the fact that I had never before advised anyone about any area of their outer life my idea that sponsorship might help would not leave me, and before we began the second healing session I relayed my idea to her. The fact that I had told her about my thoughts before the healing session was also unusual as normally any discussions would take place afterwards.

During the second healing I saw the events that had taken place more clearly. The little boy loved to fish, he had his fishing line in the water. The dog had jumped into the water and became entangled in the line. The little boy leapt in after his dog and also become caught up in the fishing line. JJ, in that life, had dived into the water in an attempt to save her child. I saw the line of her present incarnation and how she had adopted a constitution which embodied a dislike of water. Suddenly the scene changed and there, very surprisingly, was the Cambodian orphanage. Again the little boy I had seen in the boat was visible, but this time superimposed on the background scene of the orphanage. I felt that JJ would find the child she had been searching for there. The more I looked at this the more I saw, but it was still not clear. At first I observed the little blond curly-haired boy on his own. Then there was a smaller child: a girl with very dark hair with a lighter image of the boy superimposed on her. I became uncertain; did this mean a boy child, a girl child or a girl child that would lead to a boy and so perhaps two children? Had the boy child reincarnated there? Whatever it meant, the image of the boy from the fishing boat remained in the environment of the orphanage. Astonishingly, I myself was overcome with emotion and I began to cry. When I saw the child that I felt JJ could connect to I felt elated. I was overjoyed that I might be playing a part in their possible meeting, but I did not know why. I see many things when I heal but never before had I felt emotional. Such emotion left me with the desire to understand why this story had affected me as much as it had done. In a flash the orphanage scene disappeared and a third scene entered my vision. It was JJ in a later life, the JJ I had seen before holding balloons and the picture was clearer this time. It was a fairly early, I guessed around the 1930s, American fairground scene. JJ a more mature mother again with a young child; the same little boy who had been on the rowing boat previously. This second JJ had turned away from her boy for a moment to buy him some balloons; when she looked back to give him them, he had disappeared. Unknown to this JJ the child had been kidnapped by a very dark figure: a man dressed in a suit and trilby. He had been a part of an organized kidnapping and adoption gang. JJ had not been negligent but had considered herself to be so for losing her child. Her feelings of guilt had been overwhelming. I then saw a desolate

JJ being consoled by her husband of the time. They were on a cruise liner; he had taken her away on an extended holiday in an attempt to relieve her of her depression which had been triggered by her underlying emotion of guilt. Another change of scene occurred. This second JJ was in the depths of the ocean. I had a sense of her having drowned. Overwhelmed by her emotions she had committed suicide by jumping overboard. My inner eye turned to the surface of the water and there I saw several angels hovering above the spot where she was, deep under the ocean. They were beaming their light downwards into the water but were unable to find her. Right at the end of this healing session there was another dramatic shift, not only in what I was seeing, but in my own awareness. I was back to the first life, not watching it this time but there myself. This was not any sort of separation from an awareness of my own physical self sitting in my healing room; it was not a separation in any way but was the result of an expansion of my own consciousness. I was also briefly with the JJ from the first life (she had been dragged out of the lake after being unable to find her boy) and she was on the point of death. I was with her, holding her hand. Her last words had been pleading to me to "find the boy". I promised her I would.

JJ's cry for help at the end of the first life and my own promise to give that help had reverberated through all physical time. Her request for my assistance and my own willingness to give it was still alive here, in the present day. Alongside this, JJ's misplaced guilt about losing a child from both lives had permeated time and resurfaced in this lifetime. It had presented itself again in the form of her miscarriages and ensuing feelings. The pattern of pain that she was unconsciously holding onto was about the loss of the child for whom she had been responsible. This had resulted in her miscarriages, guilt and subsequent depression. Because the pain still existed within her she had recreated this reality, albeit in a less dramatic way. The loss of her dog in this life had triggered her subconscious memories of the fated fishing trip. It had awakened her unconscious impressions and compounded the guilt and depression she was already feeling over the many miscarriages. The overeating was an unsuccessful way of both attempting to suppress her painful emotions and relieve them, but it was also her means of self-punishment through the unhappiness she experienced over her weight gain. The alleviation of the effects of re-experiencing this past pain was due to her own spiritual evolution, aided by the advancement of the collective consciousness in which she was living. Inwardly, at the end of this healing, the first JJ and her child who drowned in the lake were reunited. I saw them holding hands and walking towards great light. I felt so happy that I had reunited them. This was why such strong emotions had surfaced, especially when I saw a child in the orphanage whom I felt present-day JJ might make a connection with. The experience was a powerful one for me because, finally, I had fulfilled my promise to her. After the second healing I told JJ about the two lives and that she had died in two water-related incidents. "I have a real aversion to water," was her response, "I hate it." We discussed again the sponsorship of a child and JJ told me that she had once begun to sponsor a child in Africa but had ceased doing so because something about it had not "felt right"; she had had a feeling that the child was "not the right child" for her to support.

Prior to the third healing, I constantly saw the angels searching for the second JJ who had thrown herself into the ocean. I had not told present-day JJ about them. They were unable to find her and they needed help. I had been told many years before that one of my jobs in this lifetime was to help the angelic forces. Whether I am healing or not, but especially whenever I heal, I am aware of them. I see angels as a living presence standing beside and around me. I had never accepted much of the New-Age movement and spiritual healing organizations' views on angels and their capacity. I had always felt that angels were somewhat limited in their ability, despite their fine physical existence. This was the first time I had experienced it. The angels in my vision were desperately seeking for the second JJ; they wanted to help to release her from her present depths, both physically and emotionally, but they alone did not have enough inner light, or the capacity to generate light, to be able to see her. In the third healing I would use a Transcendent light vibration to awaken JJ to her own inner Transcendent light. Once this was done, the healing she had allowed and the inner light she would begin to emit would enable the angels to find and rescue her.

During the third healing this was precisely what happened, but again my own experience expanded dramatically. As I was healing the JJ who was lying at the bottom of the ocean I suddenly found myself there too. I was in the water with her surrounded by darkness. As before, this was not a separate out-of-body experience; it was one which was totally without boundaries. I was with her in my healing room in Cambridge, while simultaneously I was deep within the ocean holding her head and awakening light within her; surrounded by deep water but feeling infinite and totally safe and secure. The difference in awareness in this healing is hard to describe, such was the loss of boundaries of time and space. Dramatically, as I was holding the second JJ's head, the darkness that was the ocean above her parted, allowing the beams of light from the angels to reach her. Having found her, these angels took hold of her and carried her upwards towards further light. I recounted the above story to present-day JJ after the healing. From her side JJ had experienced being in total darkness, in the depths of something so dark she had felt overwhelmed by it, but she had known that I was with her, helping her. She had suddenly been aware of the darkness lifting. She told me then that after her seven miscarriages she had had two significant dreams. In one of these she had been submerged in deep water, watching several patterns of light above her. She described these lights as "like swans" and had known during this dream that she had to reach them.

The continuum of individual consciousness is displayed well in JJ's story, as is the power of Transcendence to heal it. Three lives entwined, one created by another because of held emotions and their responses. Memories, albeit unconsciously, held within her physical system, impressions preventing a clear awareness. Her hidden belief in loss and distress was causing her to recreate similar scenarios and their subsequent emotions. She had been aware in the second life of what she had had to look for to heal herself and had found it in the third life. The same holding onto patterns of pain had been true for her boy, separated from his mother at a young age in at least two lives. I am reluctant to make any suggestions relating to the pictures I saw in the orphanage: what they indicated for JJ, who the child might be, and what might be the nature and potential of the relationship. It is not inconceivable, however, that the boy in some form, possibly that of a girl child, may again be waiting to be rescued. I was with her, in one way or another, in all three lives (and also in the life involving the Indian woman related later in this chapter). These lives were nothing more than a continuum in her awareness, but her evolution had brought her to the point where she felt there was a clear choice. To hold onto her hurt or to do something to release herself from it. JJ made the choice of liberation. She has now learned, and is using and enjoying, a fast and effective Transcendent technique. She has learned The Radiance Technique®. Through this, and in conjunction with other therapies, she is beginning to identify the triggers of her unwanted habitual behavior. Her consciousness-first approach, through the application of a Transcendent intermediary, has added power to her inner investigation and desire to change. It has supplied her with something which interrupts the flow of her habits, by creating within her an awareness of the connecting silent still space between her behavioral triggers and her responses. It is the experience of Transcendence that creates the opportunity for choice, the chance to alter reactions, align with evolutionary impulses, and liberate oneself from habits. What JJ both applied, in the form of her Transcendent skills, and discovered within herself from the use of them, was the pure vibration of unconditional love, and so, inner fulfillment. In short, JJ is beginning to love herself, and this is very often the last love to be realized. Changes in her behavior have come from this. Release from suffering is the result because it is impossible to knowingly abuse and deliberately harm what is truly unconditionally loved. And to love is totally fulfilling.

Early one morning some years ago I took a trip into the Sahara desert in Egypt. As I watched the sunrise over the desert I slipped into an awareness of oneness (this full state of enlightenment is described in Chapter 11). As I thought about the behavior of one of the people involved in my mid-life story I experienced completely that the basis of me was the basis of them: Transcendence. And furthermore, that someone living in this state of Transcendent Awareness would be incapable of acting from an individual egotistical level. They could only be supportive of spiritual development, in both themselves and others. I knew that when living this heightened awareness of unity the purpose behind action is solely for the unfolding of wisdom of oneness. The desire to help others heal, through their own Self-realization, emanates from the same impulse to act in spiritual self-interest. They are one and the same. Unfortunately there is a long way to go before this light and wisdom is established in the world's collective perception. I have received much help in this life from friends. But I have also encountered people who were described by the Maharishi Jyotishees (mentioned in Chapter 2) as "indirect enemies": those who purported to behave towards me in a spiritual manner and who outwardly appeared to do so, but whose impulses actually emanated from their hidden, less than spiritual, motives. Despite the distress this caused me I have now reached a state of awareness where I can be grateful for such experiences. I have finally reached the point where I can give thanks, even for some of the painful life events, which have brought me to my present consciousness. Nevertheless, this growth means I now understand that I did not need to endure them.

As I move into this new arena of expressing my experience I am aware of many past-life aspects of myself; they are still a part of me now. These different physical forms emanate from the same intention which I have projected through many different densities and vibrations. The same thought form reverberating through all physical time. The work of the past-life therapist, my own healing, and the help of two other friends who also used The Radiance Technique® provided me with much support. The result was to support me more easily in the process of incorporating a much higher vibration into my present self. This resulted in a big spiritual leap that took 20 minutes to begin and understand, and a further 6 months to increase and integrate. The vibration integrated related to two purer life aspects of myself.

Three Life Aspects

I remember many lives, far too many to mention in this book. I have spoken of a few of the traumatic ones which have colored some of my responses to situations and created reticence about speaking this truth. I also recall some which were wonderful. Integrating into the present the spiritually positive experiences of these previous life aspects is helpful. Of the happy lives, the most beautiful and positive was the life of an Indian teacher, a woman who had incarnated without all the trappings of previous experience, a curly-haired, dark-skinned child called 'Jalhandra'. Her birthplace was near what is now called Varanasi, her parents enlightened teachers of Transcendence, her life as a child spent often in the family rug shop. It was from this life the scenes (mentioned at the beginning of this chapter) of her walking along the waterside with her father came. He was also her spiritual teacher, her guru.

The parents of this child saw the purpose of her incarnation; she was raised in that life to teach spirituality and they prepared her for this role. Their enlightened status made them the perfect trainers. The personality of this teacher who was known by the name of 'Jalhandra' is one which is integrating more and more into my present physical form. There is another life aspect too and a three-pronged connection between all these bodies. That is the life aspect of my pure physical form. One day deep in meditation, as I was healing, I saw the Indian woman fall into a deep spiritual reverie. She collapsed into the total union of Nirvikalpa Samadhi. With the expansion of awareness I experienced at the same time, I cognized that it was due to the healing I was practicing in the present which had expanded her awareness too. Furthermore, that both my past- and present-life aspects were being healed and integrated further by the purest aspect which was always healing both of us. Future lives too will benefit (nevertheless there had to be acquiescence from them). The healing that I was undertaking in the present was affecting past-life forms. I was immersed in a state of total timelessness and living three lives at once. Time in this unbounded awareness did not exist.

The Indian teacher always presents herself wearing a beautiful light turquoise sari. (It is the turquoise sari that JJ saw in her first healing and it has been seen by other friends and students.) As she has integrated, her turquoise light has become a part of me; I see and feel it spreading around and outside me. Now even this life aspect is moving closer to the lighter form of my pure self. There were (and still are) three aspects of myself living within one form, three life aspects with a particular connection. There are many life aspects for everyone but, without an inner co-operation and willingness, the voices of those which are evolutionary will not be heard.

The vision an individual has of time expands with evolution until an awareness of timelessness is lived. This is known alongside the restrictions of physical time. Now that I so often perceive the Transcendence that underlies everything, I can see the previous shadows of myself as nothing more than thought forms. Sitting in meditation recently I found myself unified in a state of oneness. I was dually conscious of an inner and outer world and its connection of stillness. My perception expanded to see the incarnation lines of the people who were talking outside. They became nothing but the vibration on which they had incarnated. This line of light incorporated their predominant life desires which had brought them back to earth. Life is nothing but an expression of desire, the world a culmination of collective desires. The way they are fulfilled individually is dependent on the nature of personal karma. Only when a person's greatest desire becomes so expansive that it is, above all else, Divine Transcendence, will they begin the walk of the great liberation. This pathway in these unenlightened times is lonely, so few people are either living or determined to reach this consciousness. A friend once told me that the further along the pathway one is the narrower it gets, the less company there is, less collective support for spiritual purpose and knowing. When enough people in a society achieve the awarenesses (described in Chapter 11), this will change. More spiritual support will be available. Until then, and for always, the Avatar and a practice which provides a Transcendent intermediary will be a safe shelter. The Avatar can see the continuum of an individual's past lives as their shadows and connections. The Avatar does not love humans for the partial limited selves that they have created but in spite of them. They love the true Transcendent Self that, from their unified perception, they see. Our love of the Avatar is based on the fact that they radiate their Divinity for our healing. When the goal is finally reached there is a realization that there was no pathway and nowhere to go. It was nothing but a continuum. It was simply becoming aware.

There is no past, no future, only shadows created from mind.

11

Consciousness-First to Enlightenment

As a child I would ponder the nature of the impulses that lay behind action. In later years an inner watchfulness has on occasions observed myself displaying, to those close to me, a vulnerability. Simultaneously I inwardly knew with certainty, that vulnerable I am not. Sometimes this has been accompanied by a perception that this behavior has been nothing but the impulse of a Divine wisdom, working through me in whatever way my body could accommodate, this display of frailty being accompanied by an explanation of its cause, spiritual purpose and discussions on how pain can be transcended. At times, my behavior has appeared to me as my physical form acting as if it were nothing but an expression of the force of Transcendence, pushing into the physical arena for the purpose of teaching; for the benefit of both myself and others. The impulse of Transcendence is behind the action of everyone. This impulse will express itself through a mind and body which reflects it in its purity, or through one which is clouded by held, created denser vibrations. The world of form and its planets and their alignments, are the most extreme physical expression of a Transcendent impulse, and a reflection of individual and collective consciousness.

As previously mentioned (in Chapter 2) the biggest impetus for writing this book was what I saw as a lack, within those I met in the healing world, of any concept of enlightenment. Not only that, when used, the word enlightenment was so loosely understood that it meant nothing at all in terms of any benchmark of perceptual achievement. If ever I heard the word enlightenment mentioned, it was in relation to a post-death experience and it was never suggested it could be attained within a lifetime. At one workshop I attended, I asked the speaker when spiritual development was mentioned what they meant by the expression spiritual development. The response was that it could mean whatever someone wanted it to and it was individual. It cannot. The word enlightenment has meaning and it is applicable to everyone. Spiritual development is the integration into individual consciousness of Transcendence. There are benchmarks of development which are absolute in their definition and in this chapter I will describe some of these. Debate about whether or not higher states of awareness need to be maintained has been the kind of intellectual discussion I have witnessed. In these debates an all-encompassing liberalism about the value of any experience is replacing an understanding of experiences which fulfill spiritual purpose. The teaching of the New-Age movement today suggests that we should not live constantly in the future or the past but as much in the 'present' or 'now' as we possibly can. But (as seen in Chapter 7) the words presence and now have lost all spiritual significance. Although the teaching about the existence of presence is true they have become non-spiritual refrains, given spiritual status despite being used in a non-spiritual context. When there is a lack of awareness of the Transcendent foundation, from where we can see our thoughts come and go, this limited awareness lives with an attachment to the mind, usually the past or future. However, while current teaching is to be applauded for promoting an ideal of spiritual realization it is often deficient when it comes to technique. In its incorporation of non-spiritual practices the New-Age movement has lost the means to achieve liberation. It is fashionable at this moment in time to suggest that enlightenment should not be a pinnacle to aspire to; that we should only attempt to live in the present. It is true that Transcendence cannot be possessed. But I firmly believe the goal of enlightenment should be held in mind as the purpose of life: not as an idea that becomes a distraction, or ultimately an attachment, but as a state of consciousness that we recognize and aspire to progress towards. It is important for those within the New-Age movement to understand when a state of enlightenment is lived and when it is not. To achieve this it is necessary to have a description of the experience of enlightenment, even when it cannot, as the great Masters suggested, be fully absorbed by those not living it. There is a standard of awareness to be realized if the fullness and culmination of human existence is to be known. Complacency, and the belief of someone that they are enlightened when they are not, will be their biggest stumbling block. I have met healers whose belief that they are enlightened is fueled by their desire to be seen as someone important; to their students, healers, clients and themselves. In reality, clinging to this image of themselves as knowledgeable has prevented them from gaining real wisdom. It is essential that wisdom about the true nature of a consciousness-first approach to healing and its purpose of enlightenment permeates the healing arena. If it does not stagnation will become established. The view that imperfect vision is enlightenment, coupled with the predominant stance that enlightenment happens on its own with no regular determination needed, is unhelpful: this is often combined with many healers' practice, the movement of physical energy, which they mistakenly consider to be spiritual. The result is a recipe for stronger ego. This misunderstanding lacks the necessary ingredients of wise teaching, effective techniques and humility.

Despite never embarking upon either of the pathways – of the system or devotion (discussed in Chapter 8) – flashes of another reality may happen for some. These are usually seldom but so powerful they are never forgotten. Nearly all the descriptions of these that I have read or heard suggest that such enhanced states of awareness cannot be maintained during everyday life. But for those who practice effective awareness-enhancing techniques, these experiences do not need to be isolated life events. With the systematic use of a technique for directly accessing Transcendence they may regularly take place, and so create within an individual the experience of another reality; intermittent Transcendent Awareness. This is experienced during meditation as infinite stillness and boundless expansion. The first step towards spiritual development is to alternate between two awarenesses during meditation, through shifting a limited unenlightened perception and turning it in the direction of Transcendent Awareness. The result is the creation of a physical body and a mind which is flexible, adaptable enough to sustain an enrichment of the senses and mind which may eventually become infinite. In this process unwanted, unconscious impulses will be transmuted into a pure vibration. Spiritual development is an approach towards and an integration of Transcendence. Through regular immersion in this, the physical body and mind come to maintain and reflect more of its vibration. Perception eventually grows to acquire the realization that we are not separate from the physical world and then any psychic abilities become more penetrating and clear. An identification with Transcendence grows until individual impulses become aligned to the impulses of spiritual evolution. Shifts in desires begin to take place and, the more Transcendence is experienced, the more it is wanted. This is the same Transcendent Grace offered by the Avatar which also clears perception. The Avatar also encourages the use of systematic Transcendent meditation practices to deepen this connection further. It may not always be possible to experience the fullness of Transcendence but, as awareness of it nears, its effects are felt. Eventually the pathway of devotion becomes systematic and the pathway of the system becomes an act of devotion.

When an individual's perception reaches a certain state of refinement, material desires and their effects and ramifications no longer overshadow them. Their vision is not obscured by painful emotional patterns. They are no longer attached to the form they have created but have become identified with Transcendence. The Divine becomes the lover, the best friend. Here, when the reference point is Transcendence, is where another reality is entered: the first stage of enlightenment. My first experience of this was just after my twenty-third birthday and it is impossible to describe its immensity and clarity. I had had many spiritual experiences prior to it, but to know oneself as infinite (not only on an intellectual level, but on an *experiential* level) was phenomenal. I became eternal. I watched from within as my physical self acted out its usual routine in the arena of reactive light. It was a separate, but not out of body, inner freedom: a perception of both my inner, infinite Self, and the me that was my body, mind and emotions. An increase in inner watchfulness, and the seeming separation between Transcendence and physical, had grown from regular exposure to its vibration. But the full experience of Transcendence was quite different, so complete was the altered vision between the enlightened state and the previous clouded perception that existed before it. There are no words that adequately describe Transcendence other than it is beyond words. The experience of it is a clear disengagement from everything material, including the mind and body. Patanjali[1] describes the temporary nature of the physical mind when he says:

> The mind does not shine by its own light. It too is an object, illumined by the Self.

The inner Self has no boundaries, no thought, no attachments. Attempting to gain knowledge of it, by watching the breath and struggling to view thoughts coming and going, is a common meditation practice. True realization of the transitory nature of the mind is a *consequence* of achieving a state of Pure Awareness.

It is the establishment and sustaining of the perception I have just described that is the first stage of enlightenment. The time it takes to reach this platform will depend upon an individual's personal attachments, their karma, the purity and efficacy of the meditation system used and the depth of desire and determination for accepting Grace. Even with the help of the Avatar persistence will be important. On his deathbed Buddha encouraged his followers to work hard and make an effort to attain their enlightenment. Intensity of desire and its correlating commitment is essential. Once established in this higher awareness a place of freedom is entered. Liberated from karma; there is no more creation of it, nothing to tie them again. Individual awareness becomes Transcendent Awareness. This is being present and living in the now. When maintained during the day it is *being* the silent observer which watches the physical self, the performer of action, from within. During sleep it is *being* the silent observer of the physical self which sleeps and creates dreams. I have heard this described as similar to lucid dreaming but it is not the same. With this awareness lucid dreaming would also be silently witnessed. This is an experience like no other; it is beyond experience. To die in this state of awareness is to die liberated from the earthly desires and attachments which prompt future incarnations. Only through the impulse to help humanity would reincarnation take place. Spiritual wisdom is gained and instinctively behavior incorporates evolutionary purpose. Here, the gap that previously existed between wishes and a life which could not provide their expression is filled with inner fulfillment. Yet there are fuller states of perception beyond this to be cognized. A slight division in perception still has to be unified for greater spiritual achievement. Development does not stop here, nor do the benefits of effective meditation.

When the awareness described above has been gained, infinity has been realized, but human senses have the faculty of becoming even more refined. On the road to full enlightenment more subtle levels of physical form begin to be perceived, of both the world and its inhabitants. Inner vibrations are seen as physical structures.

Even ego may become visible. When it has been helpful for my own understanding I have observed a person's ego parading itself as their self-confidence. I have watched as an individual has projected their own fear towards others. The vibrations of an individual's confidence can be seen to come and go. My own frailties have also been observed in this way. From the first stage of enlightenment, because of what the senses see and the emotions register, the heart becomes rich in devotion. It is because of this enhancement in perception that the heart fully expands. Subtle light is visible. True love is known. Then the senses expand even more. Eventually they reach sight of the totality of oneness. I had been in the United States for a week studying The Fifth Degree of The Radiance Technique® and had been experiencing for much of that time the state of inner witnessing described above. I was also perceiving the Transcendent light part of my individual self. Light beamed out like a beacon, north, south, east and west, brilliantly, from within, the essence of me. Its quality was greater than the light I had seen previously during meditation. It was not the channeled light of spiritual healing or visualizations. Not only did I see my pure self, but I observed the original me healing directly with no prompting from any outer faculty. It appeared that my healing work was constant and I knew then that this pure aspect of me had always been teaching the healing power of Transcendence. During these experiences I was composed of three components. Transcendent Awareness observed from within, not through a restless, fickle mind but directly, both the me that was made up of its pure light vibration and my physical reactive denser light body.

The day after my return from America I went to see an Avatar in the physical form of Mother Divine and the following experience was granted through her Grace. I found myself in a state of awareness where I held within my vision the Source of creation. Completely detached from my mind, me that is the Self, which was nothing but Transcendence, perceived what had been my previous thoughts and ambitions. They were residing where I had projected them in the outer reactive light which I could also see in front of me. Created by my physical self and propelled into the world, they appeared to be invisibly suspended in the atmosphere. I saw these thoughts as spirals, pure impulses emanating from infinity (which was also me). I had placed them into the physical world, but to them I had attached the individual expectations of my small physical self. I recognized these thoughts as the base of my own world, a world which I could see beyond the 'spiral-thoughts', a world which consisted of layers of different vibrations. I distinguished which spirals related to which ideas I had had. I was aware that my real nature was not those thoughts but Transcendence. Furthermore this Transcendent Awareness was aware of itself in a totally blissful state of fulfillment. My emotions were waves of complete inner satisfaction and bliss streaming from Self to self. There was no notion of real happiness coming from the world, or from the ideas for a future I had designed. The impossibility of gaining inner peace from the desires and intentions I had created from reflected light was obvious to me. Unlike the usual moments of happiness which we have in the physical outer world, such as the special family moments and the achievements of life, this inner joy needed nothing external. Here desires were satisfied at Source. Ecstasy is the nature of such a Transcendent experience. It did not need an object, in the form of a person, item or event, from which to draw pleasure. I do not know for how long this experience lasted. By the time I left the presence of Mother Divine it had vanished, but the bliss it generated remained for nearly a week and was retained both during and outside of meditating. It was overwhelming and at times it took effort for me to speak. When I did it was from total stillness. I had entered another reality. Continuing this consciousness-first journey towards Transcendence had lead to a greater wisdom. A perception, that not only is every person's inner nature infinite, but also that their physical world is of their own making. The outcome of the higher state of consciousness related here is the cessation of desire which Buddha taught was necessary. I believe the essence of his teaching was not to subdue desires in order to reach enlightenment. It was to quell them by fulfilling them at Source *through* enlightenment. All Buddha's teaching of spiritual behavior can be viewed in the same light. What is perceived today as His routes to higher awareness (a loving understanding, kind thoughts and deeds which serve others) are all an outcome of the one pathway of Transcendence. The conduct He extolled emerges without effort from the one act of immersion in Transcendence. The same is true of Patanjali's view of a spiritual life which includes the attitude of non-violence, integrity and non-attachment. These are the *conclusion* of an awakened awareness.

Since the experience above there have been others which have nudged me towards an even greater understanding. An even more enhanced perception sees, and maintains the vision, that at the core of everything is Transcendence, both within the individual and the world they perceive. The light of Transcendence permeates it all. This is the fully enhanced state of 'oneness' that is the true awakening. The glorious state of knowing eternity. Transcendent Awareness, which perceives, is also understood as being the foundation of what is perceived. It is a realization too of a perfection and order underlying creation. When this unveiling is sustained the result is a truly harmless being. From here perception clarifies further. It expands beyond seeing the unity solely in what the gaze falls upon to a vision which encompasses oneness in everything, the culmination of this being 360° vision. Why would anyone with this wisdom of the unity of humankind randomly hurt another knowing they are so connected? Jesus[2] expressed this in the following words:

...Thou shalt love thy neighbor as thyself.

This is a good guideline for living but when He spoke Jesus was teaching about living the last state of awareness I have just detailed. It does not mean that the action of others will always be condoned, but it signifies loving them through perceiving their inner Divinity. Only when people know Transcendence, in themselves and others, will they spontaneously live this commandment. Living harmoniously is the undoubted result of spiritual development (as opposed to struggling to display peaceful conduct in order to achieve it). Bhavamukha awareness of the totality which permeates creation has been a regular occurrence for me. These experiences show me that it is possible to see God, the Divine Transcendence that is both within and without: the Source and provider of all. I taught someone to meditate recently who told me that it had changed her perception to incorporate seeing beyond what her eyes rested on in a way which had not happened before. Eventually her everyday perception will also incorporate infinity. Beyond this is Nirvikalpa Samadhi:

Nirvikalpa Samadhi

A few weeks after my twenty-third birthday I had my first taste of Nirvikalpa Samadhi. I have written about it separately, so different is it from the other states of awareness I have just described, even the awareness of oneness. To describe Nirvikalpa Samadhi as an experience is a contradiction in terms. Unlike Bhavamukha where Transcendence is known as the essence of the individual and the world that they perceive, Nirvikalpa Samadhi is beyond the mind, body and world. It transcends any notion of individuality, not even the slightest notion of an individual self exists.

During Nirvikalpa Samadhi it is not possible to think: "I am having an experience of bliss" or "I am at one". If the mind is being used it is not this state of awareness. There is no sense of a separate "I", not even one that feels it is in nirvana. This would not be possible. There is no awareness of the mind, body or surroundings.

Delving in and out of this consciousness I have seen the world disappear into Pure Awareness and reappear from it. This union can only be appreciated by the mind afterwards, understood as a experience of total oneness after the event. In Nirvikalpa Samadhi there is nothing outside Transcendence to perceive, there is only Transcendent Awareness knowing itself, Pure Awareness being itself. The experiencer is bliss, is consciousness, is infinity and nothing else. Here, no feeling of having merged exists. Individual awareness becomes Cosmic Awareness, it becomes Transcendence alone. It is not feasible to maintain this awareness and remain involved in activity as outer physical consciousness is lost and the body is inactive. Nirvikalpa Samadhi can only be sustained for any great length of time beyond this physical plane.

Nirvikalpa Samadhi is the resting place of the Avatar. When the impulses inherent within Transcendence instigate a slight separation and emerge into a physical form it is the incarnation of the Avatar. Everyone has the capacity to attain this Avataristic state.

I have heard it said, and I believe it to be true, that if an individual aspired to enlightenment as much as someone drowning wanted air it would be within their grasp. A deep yearning for this exalted state is essential. Gaining the state of enlightenment is not a random event. A strong individual ego will seek to identify itself with, and hold onto, the form of the outer world and will become attached to it. In a less-evolved state other hopes predominate. Ambitions such as becoming wealthy, famous, having status, power, intellectual brilliance or beauty are the sort of creations that the small ego obtains a feeling of "I am important" from. I once met someone who was attached to her own kindness. It is these desires and emotions, even when unconscious, which propel people into a further incarnation. They will not provide true happiness. The realization that the fulfillment of these outer experiences will never satisfy completely, that they leave one still wanting, is the first step towards becoming liberated. Reaching this realization can be a slow or fast process. The Grace of the Avatar and regular experience from Transcendent teachings will speed it up immensely.

The realities I have spoken of above are developmental yet they can and do overlap, not being so lateral as I have suggested here. Hence we read of people's perception of oneness without the prior experience of the inner witnessing state of reality and its apparent division. Many who do attain the silent observer state of reality do so during the death process. The transition between living and dying is an important connecting point where the silent space of Transcendence is more easily perceived. But this higher realization can be lived. *This is our sole purpose on earth. An individual's responsibility is to become Self-aware.* When this happens they will have a great capacity to help the rest of humanity grow in awareness. A TM teacher once told me that they had been sitting as close as two feet away from Maharishi Mahesh Yogi when he said that it was a tragedy to die in the first state of enlightenment. I was told he was completely serious and not using the tongue in cheek humor he often displayed. It seems incredible that the experience of the infinite Self can be dismissed as a loss but, from my own experiences, I understand why he made that statement. The culmination of human spiritual experience resides in the latter states I have described. Where the senses are infused with joy and gratitude at the sight of what they see. Dying in the first state of the observing consciousness, when earthly perception has not had the chance to understand its full potential, would mean missing the final state of unification, such a wonderful human possibility. The last state of awareness of oneness is a Graceful blessing; it is the blessing of Divine to Divine, the ultimate Grace bestowed by the Avatar. There is only a certain amount of spiritual growth which can be achieved alone. It is the compassionate Avatar who will unveil to an individual their real nature. Only when this goal of human spiritual development is achieved can anyone claim to be a Master.

It is from these life-events I understand that wisdom is the reflection of an individual's consciousness. My experiences include the realization that what an individual understands, and the questions they ask, are determined by the Transcendence they have integrated into their perception. Furthermore, until one knows oneself the consciousness of another cannot be understood. Every perception is real and seemingly concrete at the time of experiencing it. Only after entering higher states is previous vision (believed before the experience to be all there was) understood as less clear. A nightmare which feels real, only to be realized as a creation of the mind on waking, was used as an example of the filtering of wisdom (in Chapter 5). This analogy is worth repeating. It is similar when entering and leaving the rarefied realms which have just been described, like waking up and leaving a dream is an apt description of awakening to higher consciousness.

Most of humanity has yet to experience these states. We do not live in a spiritually determined world where our role-models are enlightened beings, but in a world of spiritual ignorance, dogma, empty rituals and abandoned truths. We inhabit a society which idolizes youth, fame, possessions and body image, rather than one which cherishes timeless wisdom; a world which dissects and analyses darkness for solutions to problems instead of introducing the light of Transcendence. There is nothing in this teaching that will prevent enjoyment of the pleasures of the outside world; they are not to be shunned. Society places much emphasis on the gratification material life provides. It is this capacity for gratification these outer forms of life are accorded, at the expense of knowing the inner real fulfillment of Transcendence, which creates dissatisfaction. A gap between desires and their satisfaction exists when Divinity within humanity is overshadowed by what it has created. Through consistently seeking gratification from material life, people can live lives of continual torment, but the pathway to the Divine is always open. The Avatar is constantly available for the dispensation of Grace whether they are in physical form or not. Their incarnation into a physical body is to help humanity know them, so humankind can hear about their possibilities. Without the incarnation of the Avatar it would be impossible for individuals to appreciate the existence of their great compassion. Moreover, the strength of humanity's attachment to the world renders an inner focus difficult. Avatars and their Transcendent teachings come in response to the suffering this causes. If humanity ceases to clutch at, and become attached to, what it does or what it has, it could live Transcendence. It is not through imagining oneself to be in this state, as unfortunately many do, that the truth is learned. I have watched teachers of supposedly higher states of consciousness encourage this sort of false activity in their course participants; misinforming them that the altered states of consciousness they are experiencing are higher states. Imagining oneself in these states is nothing but self-delusion, another created and illusory addition which has to be transcended.

I have already suggested that, with determination, routes to Divine realization are endless. Unfortunately, the majority of these are painfully slow. A consciousness-first approach is the fast way of healing, and healing is enlightenment. I have been asked how I know the difference between techniques which emanate a Transcendent vibration and those which do not. It is on the basis of the experiences I have spoken of above that I have made distinctions. The glory of this wisdom will not easily be gained through fashionable New-Age practices or dogma which contain only elements of truth, even if they have been awarded high spiritual and religious status. It will be attained through a Transcendent intermediary. Transcendence knows itself through itself alone. There is nothing more. When those who make up the world achieve Bhavamukha according to Buddha[3]:

> They have crossed over the river of sorrow.

Then, there is the complete merging into Nirvikalpa Samadhi, to the place of greatest awareness. And here, to quote Buddha[4] once more:

> When the world dissolves
> Everything becomes clear.

Purify perception to perceive what is, then it will be seen that there was nothing to purify, in reality there is nothing to transcend.

A Calling

12

La Querencia

I have begun what I came here to do; the hermit has come out of the forest. Yet still there is reticence, an uncertainty about moving from a security to a sharing consciousness. The whole of my life has been nothing but the emerging expression of a thought, a thought which has resulted in this book. Nevertheless, as I survey the finished work, I feel I am holding my fear in my hands and I have a choice: to hold onto it or to publish, begin to let it go and fulfill my outer purpose. I have illustrated my understanding based on my present perception and experience. I have been teaching about Transcendence since the first of my incarnations and in many of them was prevented from continuing; when individual and collective consciousness was less expanded this wisdom was deemed to be heretical. Because I held the pain from those past experiences in this life, I personally helped to recreate the same scenarios, giving all concerned the opportunity to display old behavior or to change their emotional response patterns. There are no victims, only a conscious or unconscious willingness to participate which emanates from a variety of motives. Today resistance still presents itself, but the expansion in the collective awareness ensures it appears in a different form and its sanctions are less physically damaging. Why do I think that there will be more interest in what I am saying this time? There is the start of an increase in awareness in parts of the world, resulting in a small peak of people with wisdom about the hidden nature of life and a larger number of people wishing to investigate it. I believe that the time will come when householders have access to this knowledge in a way which has not happened before. But this could still take millennia. To facilitate it the teachers of the future will teach more versatile techniques with greater powers of expansion. Awareness always grows and at this time there is preparation for further shifts in human consciousness. It is for this reason that today a handful of householder teachers who know the enlightened state have come to prominence. They will show the possibilities to other householders. I do not believe this change will happen solely from the use of the spiritual healing and reiki practices that I have seen so far. It will need a purer, more profound and more versatile practice. Real change will come from the use and effects of a deeper wisdom.

The investigation of outer form undertaken by science has brought comfort to our lives but its findings have been influenced by factors other than its own enquiry. Science is a reflection of the collective awareness. Its paradigms constantly change in accordance with this consciousness but even now there is evidence of a physical unity. The rigor of scientific investigation undertaken so far by physicists tells us that the matter that forms the human body was once the matter of the universe. We are literally stardust. The world used to be one land mass that broke apart, creating the foundation for physical and cultural difference. According to current theory the species that became modern humanity emanated from one race in Africa and diversified. People have been forced, though physical expansion, to at least attempt to live in harmony. Medical science tells us that the human eye has developed so well it is able to perceive diversity where other species only see shadows. Darwin taught us about the capacity of the physical form to adapt and change, suggesting at some level there is an underlying similarity. Scientists have discovered the space between particles. They talk about space being connected but that this connectivity has yet to be seen. Network science looks for links and is finding them between the genes that cause disease; it is uncovering connections not thought possible only a few years ago. Some scientists claim that all major advances will be based on the discovery of networks and underlying links. Physicists now say that subatomic particles behave differently when under supervision, displaying an invisible connection between what is observed and the observer.

As I write these words I have just heard a scientist* claim that if the title 'creationist' was removed, and replaced with the description 'design', scientifically unacceptable theories of human development would become palatable to science. There is no doubt that rigorous investigation by future scientists will reveal new levels of physical creation and hidden universal laws of nature. The potential to use solely the vibration of thought as a means of human communication will be uncovered and utilized, along with a greater understanding of the nature of light. They will find even more intelligent structures which underpin matter and when scientists perceive the fastest vibration of all they will know stillness. These discoveries will be applied by medical scientists to utilize finer vibrations of light for the benefit of humanity. In a more compassionate time medicine will be less driven by financial expediency and reflect more concern for comfort and care. This fusing of rigorous investigation and empathy will assist in releasing humankind from suffering and will be a reflection of the growth and melding of science and spirituality. The spiritual hierarchy (described in Chapter 3) is nothing more than a finer physical structure from Transcendence to ensure that Grace and wisdom cascade through denser form. Its purpose is to show the whole of humanity its opportunity to become aware of its Transcendent Source; to teach it about the possibility of complete union. It is the function of the hierarchy to call you, the individual spark that you are, to your ultimate experience. Without this Divinely given individuality the question: "Who am I?" could not be asked.

You have heard what the New-Age in its infancy has to offer and no doubt experienced its benefits. I question, however, if it has brought you to a direct experience of Transcendence. I have just looked at another New-Age article that waxed lyrical about the existence of a unifying principle, but showed neither experience of it, nor a direct route to it. With its eclectic make-up the New-Age movement has lost its way. The anticipated liberalism of its members (anticipated because having a liberal stance is considered to be a spiritual stance) has resulted in a subtle form of repression. Criticism is perceived as unspiritual and has been limited. Years ago I was offered a room in a local complementary therapy center. When I told my interviewer that with The Radiance Technique® I was practicing the complete, intact, seven-level system of universal Radiant energy that was both authentic and transcendental, there was a sharp intake of breath. This clearly suggested that I should not be speaking of my technique as if it were different to other reiki techniques. My reaction was that I must study to levels which did not exist among reiki healers in order to gain outer credibility. I also refused the offer of the healing room, resulting in a further restriction for the expression of this wisdom. It had been my choice. My old patterns encouraged by collective resistance had predominated. An all-inclusive New-Age attitude exists which has meant a lack of discernment, standards and efficacy. Furthermore, this cannot be spoken of for fear of upsetting its all-encompassing viewpoint. It is time for this to change. Spiritual discrimination needs to be applied and standards set. I know two things only:

- The first is that that I must keep talking of this wisdom, irrespective of whether or not anyone listens.

- The second: that the states of awareness I have spoken of are a possibility for you all. If you want them, and, if you use the fastest means available, you will stand a better chance of achieving them.

At the beginning of this journey you will need an intermediary so make it Transcendence. Time you spend in deep Transcendent meditation is invaluable. Reaching Divine Awareness needs a desire so intense it overrules everything else. By this I do not mean that it is necessary to abandon all your responsibilities. If, in this life, your responsibility is to your children, then that must be accepted. Bringing up your children is your choice, your karma and your service to society. But, in the process of doing this, you will need to create a relationship with God; thus your service to your family and your children becomes spiritual. Human love can be elevated to the status of Divine love. The kind of teachings I have spoken of will make this easier for you. If you are unable to make a connection with the Godhead create one with the Avatar. Make use of the Avatar, visit them with an inner willingness to change and receive their Grace. If you cannot visit them repeat their name, speak to them inwardly and they will hear you. Ask them for release from your suffering, not just in the shape of a better physical life, but in the form of inner liberation, and improvements in life will come from this. The form of the present physical body is dense and may never be perfect. Nevertheless ask the Avatar for a cessation of your pain with the same intensity you would if you were asking for a loved one who was ill to become well. Ask them for your liberation from your attachment to the world of phenomena and form which, due to its transient nature, will never fulfill you. This world can be enjoyed without it overshadowing your true nature. Place yourself within their radar and when their attention is placed on you it will purify you. If your inclination to know the Avatar has not been ignited, the experience of a technique with a vibration directly from Transcendence will do this for you. Practice a transcendent healing and meditation and it will awaken a desire in you for more. When you are 'ripe' the Avatar will bestow spiritual abundance and power onto you. Jesus[1] said:

> ...I am the way, the truth, and the life: no man cometh unto the Father, but by me.

Jesus was referring to His Transcendent nature. No individual reaches an awareness of Transcendence other than through Transcendence itself. All Avatars, or one who has attained Avataristic status, have this capacity. The experience of its Grace will come to you a thousand times more quickly when you genuinely desire and demand it. This is how it works: in particular, healers, those who claim to know about healing light and its effects, have a responsibility to learn about the difference between pure Transcendent light and denser, outer reactive light. They must begin to use the former for the benefit of both themselves and their clients. No great teacher ever suggested merely the investigation of physical form as a route to Divine realization, either of the world or an individual's. Trying to understand the world at the expense of knowing the inner Self is futile and a pathway abounding in obstacles. Many who take this route fail. The successful claims made on behalf of these types of investigative practices are based on a pre-existing expansion of consciousness which is the real instigator of physical change. Jesus,[2] when talking of a consciousness-first approach said:

> But seek ye first the kingdom of God...

When a choice is made to incorporate the impulses of spiritual evolution into behavior action becomes harmless and in the best interests of all concerned. Then you will truly serve humanity. The collective awareness of the world, its laws, animal kingdom and suffering is dependent on the awareness of individuals within it. The same is true of the New-Age movement. If those who make up the present force of the New-Age adopt a consciousness-first approach it will take the movement out of its infancy into its adolescence. It is not enough to talk about ideals of peace and unity. Real peace is not a lack of war or conflict; it is living the vibration inner peace.

'La querencia' are Spanish words; the translation would probably be 'the homecoming'. Querencia comes from the verb 'querer' to desire, a verb which sometimes carries the sense of accepting a challenge. In Spanish la querencia also refers to a place on the ground where one feels secure, a place from which one's strength is drawn. In Spain querencia is often used to describe the spot in a bullring where the bull goes to strengthen and embolden itself in preparation for its encounters with the picadors and banderilleros.** It is also a word which describes a place within ourselves that is a safe haven, somewhere deep inside us where we know who we really are and from where we express our true beliefs. Our real querencia is Transcendence. It is at one time our destination, our home, our true Selves. The mention of the wounded bull will give rise to thoughts of death; this is intentional. The single most important thing you will do in this lifetime is to die. Within that moment you will be the sum of who you are, all your life aspects together. It is this which determines the expansion or limitation of your awareness, and, if you have not already reached a state of enlightenment, you will find out if you have grown enough to attain it. Presently, Transcendent Awareness is most often reached during the dying process. Some of you will reach it at the ending of your lives. But it is better to *live* it and know the wondrous glory of human existence. Don't feel satisfied if you have slipped in and out of this state of awareness, don't wait for your deathbed experience where this great opportunity may be missed. Establish yourself in infinity while alive. The experience of enlightenment is within your grasp, here and now. It is the pinnacle of human evolution and what we were born to live in. Only then as

Patanjali[3/4] says:

> All confusion about the nature of the Self vanishes for one who has seen its glory.

And

> Now the process by which evolution unfolds through time is understood.

Only when enlightened is it legitimate to use the exalted title of Master. The inherent, evolutionary support of the Divine will always edge you towards this goal but the choice is yours. The Avatars and teachers are calling you. They have never moved, you have simply ceased to recognize them. There are no guarantees except the promise you elicit from them, but you must agree to change. It would be tragic to remain the unfulfilled rosebud and not make a tremendous effort to flower. The true Avatar will protect you and when you are ready grant you the ultimate experience. Take refuge in them; the quality of your life and your enlightenment ultimately depend on their Grace. The Grace of the Avatar is entwined into the Transcendent system and such practices will lead you towards them. In doing so devotion and the system will be combined. The light of the Avatar will shine through the dark dream that is your suffering; they will take you under their wing and never deny you help. Only the Avatar can grant you your final Grace of oneness, Transcendent Awareness bestowing the ultimate blessing on itself. But the rest is in your hands. Your spiritual development is ultimately your responsibility. Don't in some future life analyze this life as a lost possibility. Begin your magic carpet ride now; at the least what you gain in this life will create evolutionary impulses for future lives. It will raise the vibration behind your last thought, and it is this last thought in conjunction with its motivating emotion, which will set the stage for your future existence. The Divine does not mind your errors of judgment, only your complacency. The Vedas[5] speak of a Transcendent Source which created the diversity of the world in thousands of physical forms, then hiding Transcendence within it, unable to be seen, heard, touched, tasted or smelled. When you realize the goal, you will find it was not hidden at all, you simply had to look.

Not long ago I was granted an interview with Mother Divine in one of her physical incarnations; She told me to publish this book with Her blessing. Later She called me Her daughter 'Jalhandra'. After speaking with her, during meditation, I saw my inner spiritual eye being purified further by fire. Shortly afterwards it cleared, as if curtains that had hung across it were parted. I moved into an awareness in which I saw the whole of creation from Transcendence. My Transcendent Self was the Source of all I was perceiving. I understood my physical and spiritual connection to this particular incarnation of Mother Divine, saw my spiritual family and my worldly responsibility. A moment of creation was revealed. Everything and everyone within my vision – animals, children, adults – were in that moment, all my children. This continued as I opened my eyes and watched people walking around the room. Soon afterwards I was with nearly a hundred people, we were using together The Advanced Degrees of The Radiance Technique®. I slipped again into Nirvikalpa Samadhi. The room and those in it dissolved into Transcendence. At the feet of the Divine, either in the form of a Transcendent teaching or the Avatar is a crossroads. Hearing wisdom and its vibration will shake you and create within you an awakening possibility. During this process you will decide, consciously or not, whether to move with the flow of evolution or cling harder to your individual ego and to the illusory identity and form you have created. The very fact that you are reading this book means that you are searching. In reading it there is an awakening opportunity after which a decision will be made to accept or reject what has been read. I have seen this vibration of awakening remain in people for weeks, being reinvigorated at the sound of the repeated teaching. I have also seen it rejected in the blink of an eye. If you are not living the states of consciousness (spoken of in Chapter 11) then every one of your past-life aspects, the thought forms you have expressed, has been an unrealized opportunity. This book has been written on behalf of the Divine, and as you are absorbing it, you have a choice: a chance to move towards liberation. I am inviting you now to go beyond the place from where you began this journey, to walk across the bridge of love towards the total union which is your great possibility. Guru Dev[6], the Master who taught and prepared Maharishi, encouraged effort. May His words ring loud and clear and remain within your memory until you reach this goal:

> To get a human body is a rare thing. Make full use of it. There are 8,400,000 kinds of lives which a soul can gather. After that one gets a chance to be human, to get a human body. Therefore, one should not waste this chance. Every second in human life is very valuable. If you don't value this, then you will have nothing in hand and you will weep in the end. Because you are human, God has given you the power to think and decide what is good and bad. Therefore you can do the best possible action. You should never consider yourself weak or a fallen creature. Whatever may have happened up to now may be because you didn't know, but now be careful. After getting a human body if you don't find God, then you have sold a diamond for the price of spinach.

Now you know.

Jalhandra

The surge of evolution is relentless, interfere with its unfolding and you will be like a bud which fails to flower. From the viewpoint of the Absolute this is an acceptable part of the process, from the viewpoint of the individual it is tragic.

References

Chapter 2

1. *Ramakrishna and His Disciples* – Christopher Isherwood – Page 118 – Shepheard-Walwyn (Publishers) Ltd – 1986. (First published as a hardback by Methuen, 1965)
2. *The Vedas* – Said to be the oldest records of knowledge of the fullness of life and thought to be brought to north-west India by the Aryan civilization, although this is not certain. They contain truths cognized by enlightened seers at the beginning of time. Traditionally passed down orally, in written form they are still the sacred texts of Hinduism.

Chapter 3

1. *The Vedas* – Said to be the oldest records of knowledge of the fullness of life and thought to be brought to north-west India by the Aryan civilization, although this is not certain. They contain truths cognized by enlightened seers at the beginning of time. Traditionally passed down orally, in written form they are still the sacred texts of Hinduism.
2. *The Holy Bible,* King James Version – The Gospel According to St. John – Chapter 1, Verse 1
3. *The Holy Bible,* King James Version – Genesis – Chapter 1, Verse 3
4. *Ramakrishna and His Disciples* – Christopher Isherwood – Page 199 – Shepheard-Walwyn (Publishers) Ltd – 1986. (First published as a hardback by Methuen, 1965)
5. *Ramakrishna and His Disciples* – Christopher Isherwood – Page 123 – Shepheard-Walwyn (Publishers) Ltd – 1986. (First published as a hardback by Methuen, 1965)
6. *The Dhammapada* – The Sayings of the Buddha – 21. Out of the Forest – Page 99 – Translated by Thomas Byrom – Rider, an imprint of Edbury Publishing, 2002. This edition by Rider, 2008.

7. *The Dhammapada* – The Sayings of the Buddha – 6. The Wise Man – Page 44 – Translated by Thomas Byrom – Rider, an imprint of Edbury Publishing, 2002. This edition by Rider, 2008.

Chapter 4

1. *The Dhammapada* – The Sayings of the Buddha – 6. The Wise Man – Page 43 – Translated by Thomas Byrom – Rider, an imprint of Edbury Publishing, 2002. This edition by Rider, 2008.
2. *The Essential Aurobindo* – Edited with an introduction and new afterword by Robert A. McDermott – Page 59 – Lindisfarne Press, 1987
3. *The Vedas* – Said to be the oldest records of knowledge of the fullness of life and thought to be brought to north-west India by the Aryan civilization, although this is not certain. They contain truths cognized by enlightened seers at the beginning of time. Traditionally passed down orally, in written form they are still the sacred texts of Hinduism.
4. *The Holy Bible*, King James Version – The Gospel According to St. Luke – Chapter 17, Verse 21

Chapter 5

1. *The Vedas* – Said to be the oldest records of knowledge of the fullness of life and thought to be brought to north-west India by the Aryan civilization, although this is not certain. They contain truths cognized by enlightened seers at the beginning of time. Traditionally passed down orally, in written form they are still the sacred texts of Hinduism.
2. *Effortless Being: The Yoga Sutras of Patanjali* – Treading the Path Verse 12 – Page 74 –Translated by Alistair Shearer – Wildwood House Ltd, 1982

Chapter 6

1. *The Essential Aurobindo* – Edited with an introduction and new afterword by Robert A. McDermott – Page 25 of the Introduction – Lindisfarne Press, 1987
2. *The Maharishi* – Paul Mason – Page 199 and Page 162 – Element Books Ltd – 1994 – Quotes transcribed from public discourses taped by members of the audience.

Chapter 7

1. *Effortless Being: The Yoga Sutras of Patanjali* – Expansion Verse 51 – Page 112 – Translated by Alistair Shearer – Wildwood House Ltd, 1982
2. *Ramakrishna and His Disciples* – Christopher Isherwood – Page 91 – Shepheard-Walwyn (Publishers) Ltd – 1986. (First published as a hardback by Methuen, 1965)
3. *Ramakrishna and His Disciples* – Christopher Isherwood – Page 221 – Shepheard-Walwyn (Publishers) Ltd – 1986. (First published as a hardback by Methuen, 1965)
4. *The Essential Aurobindo* – Edited with an introduction and new afterword by Robert A. McDermott – Page 69 – Lindisfarne Press, 1987
5. *The Daily Telegraph* – "Westerners are too self-absorbed" – Interview with the Dalai Lama – Alice Thomson – From Saturday April 1st 2006 – Page 17

Chapter 8

1. *Effortless Being: The Yoga Sutras of Patanjali* – Expansion Verse 55 – Page 112 – Translated by Alistair Shearer – Wildwood House Ltd, 1982

Chapter 11

1. *Effortless Being: The Yoga Sutras of Patanjali* – Enlightenment Verse 19 – Page 119 – Translated by Alistair Shearer – Wildwood House Ltd, 1982

2. *The Holy Bible*, King James Version – The Gospel According to St. Mark – Chapter 12, Verse 31
3. *The Dhammapada* – The Sayings of the Buddha – 14. The Man Who is Awake – Page 73 – Translated by Thomas Byrom – Rider, an imprint of Edbury Publishing, 2002. This edition by Rider, 2008.
4. *The Dhammapada* – The Sayings of the Buddha – 26. The True Master – Page 123 – Translated by Thomas Byrom – Rider, an imprint of Edbury Publishing, 2002. This edition by Rider, 2008.

Chapter 12

1. *The Holy Bible*, King James Version – The Gospel According to St. John – Chapter 14, Verse 6
2. *The Holy Bible*, King James Version – The Gospel According to St. Matthew – The Sermon on the Mount – Chapter 6, Verse 33
3. *Effortless Being: The Yoga Sutras of Patanjali* – Enlightenment Verse 25 – Page 121 – Translated by Alistair Shearer – Wildwood House Ltd, 1982
4. *Effortless Being: The Yoga Sutras of Patanjali* – Enlightenment Verse 33 – Page 124 – Translated by Alistair Shearer – Wildwood House Ltd, 1982
5. *The Vedas* – Said to be the oldest records of knowledge of the fullness of life and thought to be brought to north-west India by the Aryan civilization, although this is not certain. They contain truths cognized by enlightened seers at the beginning of time. Traditionally passed down orally, in written form they are still the sacred texts of Hinduism.
6. *The 108 Teachings of Guru Dev – Teaching No. 59* – Public discourse recorded in Rishikesh, February, 1969 – translator unknown.

* Name unknown

** Source unknown

Glossary

Avatar – Is a direct incarnation of Divine consciousness into physical form. They have no karma other than the desire to release humanity from its suffering.

Ayurveda – Means knowledge of lifespan. Correctly applied it is the ancient wisdom of understanding influences on the body. In Ayurveda some food is viewed as medicinal.

Bhavamukha – A state of enlightenment in which awareness of both the physical world and Transcendence is maintained simultaneously. A lesser state than Nirvikalpa Samadhi where awareness is withdrawn from the world.

Brahman – The Wholeness.

Chakras or Energy Centers – Energy centers connecting the physical body with the transcendent and the vibrations in-between. The location of the seven main energy centers on the body are well documented. Much emphasis is given in spiritual healing circles to "balancing" the chakras of the person being healed and healers often visualize opening their own in order to channel "healing energies".

Darshan – The blessing and display of the Self-realized, their presence is the Grace that purifies. To be in their company is to receive their darshan.

Householder – Those who are born to be engaged in everyday life, unlike those born to live as monks.

Jyotish / Jyotishees – Jyotish is the skill of foreseeing future trends and events and alleviating difficulties. Mathematically calculated from the *exact* time of birth, the art of restructuring action to become spiritually evolutionary. (Maharishi Jyotishees were those who were approved by Maharishi to give Jyotish readings to members of the TM movement.)

Karma / Karmic – There is no such thing as luck, only our actions and their consequences. From desire to thought to action we create and this creation affects us in return. This is our karma. The state of enlightenment is a state of liberation from these effects and ramifications of our action; it is freedom from karma.

Kundalini – Said to be a center of energy at the base of the spine. Rousing this energy to rise up through the body was a popular spiritual practice some years ago and has been well documented for its detrimental side-effects when kundalini energy enters an energy center which is totally unprepared for it.

Nirvikalpa Samadhi – When the perceiver, the process of perceiving and what is perceived become the same; individual identity is dissolved into Pure Awareness. They become one and the same. There is no sense of 'I'. This awareness is maintained only beyond the dense physical plane. In this state of consciousness the world is experienced simply as infinity and bliss.

The Shankaracharya Order – Traditionally the custodians of Vedic wisdom in India and its philosophy of union and effective means of achieving it.